HOW TO
TEACH
YOUR
BABY
TO READ

The Better Baby Press

8801 Stenton Avenue
Philadelphia, Pennsylvania 19118

HOW TO
TEACH
YOUR
BABY
TO READ

THE
GENTLE
REVOLUTION

by Glenn Doman

The author wishes to thank the following publishers for their kind permission to quote from copyright material:

Newsweek, Vol. LXI No. 19 (May 13, 1963), p. 96.

The Bobbs-Merrill Company, Inc., for excerpts from *Natural Education* by Winifred Sackville Stoner, copyright 1914 by The Bobbs-Merrill Company, 1942 by Winifred Stoner Gordon.

Stanford University Press, for excerpts from *The Promise of Youth: Follow-up Studies of a Thousand Gifted Children, Genetic Studies of Genius,* Volume III, by Barbara Stoddard Burks, Dortha Williams Jensen, and Lewis M. Terman (Stanford: Stanford University Press, 1930), pp. 248–50.

Harvard University Press, for brief quotation from Plato's *Republic,* translated by Paul Shorey (the Loeb Classical Library; Harvard University Press), p. 624.

Saturday Review, for brief excerpts from an article by John Ciardi, entitled "When Do They Know Too Much?" (May 11, 1963).

Jacket cover pictures are of
E.T.I. mother and child,
Mrs. Gloria Sherman and Jason,
of Philadelphia, Pa.
Photographer: Jim Kaliss

This book is respectfully dedicated to my wife, Hazel Doman, who, through their mothers, has taught hundreds of one-, two- and three-year-old brain-injured children *to enjoy reading.*

It is also dedicated to four men who, each in his own way, made this work and this book possible:
Samuel M. Henshaw
A. Vinton Clarke
Temple Fay
Jay Cooke
They left giant footprints across the world they trod and deep impressions in our minds and hearts.

WORKS BY THE AUTHOR.

GENTLE REVOLUTION SERIES:
* How to Teach Your Baby to Read
* Teach Your Baby Math
* What to Do About Your Brain-Injured Child

CHILDREN'S BOOK:
Nose is Not Toes

FORTHCOMING TITLE:
How to Multiply Your Baby's Intelligence.

GENTLE REVOLUTION KIT SERIES:
* How to Teach Your Baby to Read Kits
* How to Teach Your Baby Math Kits

foreword

Beginning a project in clinical research is like getting on a train with an unknown destination. It's full of mystery and excitement but you never know whether you'll have a compartment or be going third class, whether the train has a diner or not, whether the trip will cost a dollar or all you've got and, most of all, whether you are going to end up where you intended or in a foreign place you never dreamed of visiting.

When our team members got on this train at the various stations, we were hoping that our destination was better treatment for severely brain-injured children. None of us dreamed that if we achieved that goal, we would stay right on the train till we reached a place where brain-injured children might even be made superior to unhurt children.

The trip has thus far taken twenty years, and the accommodations were third class, the diner served mostly sandwiches, night after night, often at three in the morning. The tickets cost all we had, some of us did not live long enough to finish the trip—and none of us would have missed it for anything else the world has to offer. It's been a fascinating trip.

The original passenger list included a brain surgeon, a physiatrist (an M.D. who specializes in physical medicine and rehabilitation), a physical therapist, a speech therapist, a psychologist, an educator and a nurse. Now there are more than a hundred of us all told, with many additional kinds of specialists.

The little team was formed originally because each of us was individually charged with some phase of the treatment of severely brain-injured children—and each of us individually was failing.

If you are going to choose a creative field in which to work, it is difficult to pick one with more room for improvement than one in which failure has been one hundred per cent and success is non-existent.

When we began our work together twenty years ago *we had never seen, or heard of, a single brain-injured child who had ever got well.*

The group that formed after our individual failures would today be called a rehabilitation team. In those days so long ago neither of those words were fashionable and we looked upon ourselves as nothing so grand as all that. Perhaps we saw ourselves more pathetically and more clearly as a group who had banded together, much as a convoy does, hoping that we would be stronger together than we had proved to be separately.

We began by attacking the most basic problem which faced those who dealt with brain-injured children two decades ago. This problem was *identification*. There were three very different kinds of children with problems who were invariably mixed together as if they were the same. The fact is that they were not even ninety-second cousins. They got lumped together in those days (and, tragically, they still are in much of the world) for the very poor reason that they frequently look, and sometimes act, the same.

The three kinds of children who were constantly put together were deficient children with brains which were qualitatively and quantitatively inferior, psychotic children with physically *normal* brains but unsound minds, and finally truly brain-injured children who had good brains but which had been physically hurt.

We were concerned only with the last type of children, who had suffered injuries to a brain which at conception was perfectly good. We came to learn that although the truly deficient child and the truly psychotic child were comparatively few in number, hundreds of thousands of children were, and are, diagnosed as deficient or psychotic, while they were actually brain-injured children. Generally such mistaken diagnosis came about because many of the brain-injured children incurred injuries to a good brain before they were born.

When we had learned, after many years of work in the operating room and at the bedside, which children were truly brain-injured we could then begin to attack the problem itself—the injured brain.

We discovered that it mattered very little (except from a research point of view) whether a child had incurred his injury prenatally, at the instant of birth, or postnatally. This was rather like being concerned about whether a child had been hit by an automobile before noon, at noon or after noon. What really mattered was which part of his brain had been hurt, how much it had been hurt, and what might be done about it.

We discovered further that it mattered very little whether a child's good brain had been hurt as a result of his parents having an incompatible Rh factor, his mother having had an infectious disease such as German measles during the first three months of pregnancy, insufficient oxygen having reached his brain during the prenatal period, or because he had been born prematurely. The brain can also be hurt as a result of protracted labor, by the child's falling on his head at two months of age and suffering blood clots on his brain, by having a high temperature with encephalitis at three years of age, by being struck by an automobile at five years of age, or by any of a hundred other factors.

Again, while this was significant from the research point of view, it was rather like worrying about whether a particular child had been hit by a car or a hammer. The important thing here was which part of the child's brain was hurt, how much it was hurt, and what we were going to do about it.

In those early days, the world that dealt with brain-injured children held the view that the problems of these children might be solved by treating the symptoms which existed in the ears, eyes, nose, mouth, chest, shoulders, elbows, wrist, fingers, hips, knees, ankles and toes. A large portion of the world still believes this today.

Such an approach did not work then and could not possibly work.

Because of this total lack of success, we concluded that if we were to solve the multiple symptoms of the brain-injured child we would have to attack the source of the problem and approach the human brain itself.

While at first this seemed an impossible or at least monumental task, in the years that followed we and others found both surgical and nonsurgical methods of treating the brain itself.

We held the simple belief that to treat the symptoms of an illness or injury, and to expect the disease to disappear, was unmedical, unscientific and irrational, and if all these reasons were not enough to make us abandon such an attack, then the simple fact remained that brain-injured children approached in such a manner never got well.

On the contrary, we felt that if we could attack the problem itself, the symptoms would disappear spontaneously to the exact extent of our success in dealing with the injury in the brain itself.

First we tackled the problem from a nonsurgical standpoint. In the years that followed, we became persuaded that if we could hope to succeed with the hurt brain itself, we would have to find ways to reproduce in some manner the neurological growth patterns of a well child. This meant understanding how a well child's brain begins, grows and matures. We studied intently many hundreds of well newborn babies, infants and children. We studied them very carefully.

As we learned what normal brain growth is and means we began to find that the simple and long-known basic activities of well children, such as crawling and creeping, are of the greatest possible importance to the brain. We learned that if such activities are denied well children, because of cultural, environmental or social factors, their potential is severely limited. The potential of brain-injured children is even more affected.

As we learned more about ways to reproduce this normal physical pattern of growing up we began to see brain-injured children improve— ever so slightly.

It was at about this time that the neurosurgical components of our team began to prove conclusively that the answer lay in the brain itself, by developing successful surgical approaches to it. There were certain types of brain-injured children whose problems were of a progressive nature, and these children had consistently died early. Chief among these were the hydrocephalics, the children with "water on the brain." Such children had huge heads due to the pressure of cerebrospinal fluid which could not be resorbed in the normal manner due to their injuries. Nevertheless the fluid continued to be created as in normal people.

No one had ever been quite so foolish as to try to treat the symptoms of this disease by massage or exercise or braces. As the pressure on the brain increased these children had always died. Our neurosurgeon, working with an engineer, developed a tube which carried the excess cerebrospinal fluid from the reservoirs called the ventricles, deep inside the human brain, to the jugular vein and thus into the blood stream, where it could be resorbed in the normal manner. This tube had within it an ingenious valve which would permit the excess fluid to flow outward while simultaneously preventing the blood from flowing back into the brain.

This almost magical device was surgically implanted within the brain and was called "the V-J shunt." There are twenty-five thousand children in the world today who would not be alive, were it not for this simple tube. Many of these children are living completely normal lives and go to school with well children.

Here was beautiful evidence of the complete futility of attacking the symptoms of brain injury, as well as the unassailable logic and necessity for treating the hurt brain itself.

Another startling method will serve as an example of the many types of successful brain surgery which are in use today to solve the problems of the brain-injured child.

There are actually two brains, a right brain and a left brain. These two brains are divided right down the middle of the head from front to rear. In well human beings the right brain (or, if you like, the right half of the brain) is responsible for controlling the left side of the body, while the left half of the brain is responsible for running the right side of the body.

If one half of the brain is hurt to any large degree, the results are catastrophic. The opposite side of the body will be paralyzed, the child will be severely restricted in all functions. Many such children have constant, severe and convulsive seizures which do not respond to any known medication.

It need hardly be said that such children also die.

The ancient cry of those who stood for doing

nothing had been chanted over and over for decades. "When a brain cell is dead it is dead and nothing can be done for children with dead brain cells, so don't try." But by 1955 the neurosurgical members of our group were performing an almost unbelievable kind of surgery on such children; it is called hemispherectomy.

Hemispherectomy is precisely what that name implies—the surgical removal of half of the human brain.

Now we saw children with half a brain in the head and with the other half, billions of brain cells, in a jar at the hospital—dead and gone. But the children were not dead.

Instead we saw children with only half a brain who walked, talked and went to school like other children. *Several such children were above average, and at least one of them had an I.Q. in the genius area.*

It was now obvious that if one half of a child's brain was seriously hurt, it mattered little how good the other half was as long as the hurt half remained. If, for example, such a child was suffering convulsions caused by the injured left brain, he would be unable to demonstrate his function or intelligence until that half was removed in order to let the intact right brain take over the entire function without interference.

We had long held that, contrary to popular belief, a child might have ten dead brain cells and we would not even know it. Perhaps, we said, he might have a hundred dead brain cells, and we would not be aware of it. Perhaps, we said, even a thousand.

Not in our wildest dreams had we dared to believe that a child might have *billions* of dead brain cells and yet perform almost as well and sometimes even better than an average child.

Now the reader must join us in a speculation. How long could we look at Johnny, who had half his brain removed, and see him perform as well as Billy, who had an intact brain, without asking the question, "What is wrong with *Billy*?" Why did not Billy, who had twice as much brain as Johnny, perform twice as well or at least better?

Having seen this happen over and over again we began to look with new and questioning eyes at average children.

Were average children doing as well as they might? Here was an important question we had never dreamed of asking.

In the meantime, the nonsurgical elements of the team had acquired a great deal more knowledge of how such children grow and how their brains develop. As our knowledge of normality increased, our simple methods for reproducing that normality in brain-injured children kept pace. By now we were beginning to see a small number of brain-injured children reach wellness by the use of the simple nonsurgical methods of treatment which were steadily evolving and improving.

It is not the purpose of this book to detail either the concepts or the methods used to solve the multiple problems of brain-injured children. Other books, which are already published or which are presently in manuscript form, deal with the treatment of the brain-injured child. However, the fact that this is being accomplished daily is of significance in understanding the pathway which led to the knowledge that well children can perform infinitely better than they are doing at present. It is sufficient to say that extremely simple techniques were devised to reproduce the patterns of normal development in brain-injured children.

As an example, when a brain-injured child is unable to move correctly he is simply taken in an orderly progression through the stages of growth which occur in well children. First he is helped to move his arms and legs, then to crawl, then to creep, then finally to walk. He is physically aided in doing these things in a patterned sequence. He progresses through these ever higher stages in the same manner as a child does in the grades at school, and is given unlimited opportunity to utilize these activities.

Soon we began to see severely brain-injured

children whose performance rivaled that of children who had not suffered a brain injury.

As these techniques improved even more, we began to see brain-injured children emerge who could not only perform as well as average children but, indeed, who could not be distinguished from them.

As our understanding of neurological growth and normality began to assume a really clear pattern, and as methods for the recapitulation of normality multiplied, *we even began to see some brain-injured children who performed at above average, or even superior, levels.*

It was exciting beyond measure. It was even a little bit frightening. It seemed clear that we had, at the very least, underestimated every child's potential.

This raised a fascinating question. Suppose we looked at three seven-year-old children: Albert, who had half his brain in the jar; Billy who had a perfectly normal brain; and Charley who had been treated nonsurgically and who now performed in a totally normal way, although he still had millions of dead cells in his brain.

Albert, with half his brain gone, was as intelligent as Billy. So was Charley, with millions of dead cells in his head.

What was wrong with nice, average, unhurt Billy?

What was wrong with *well* children?

For years our work had been charged with the vibrancy that one feels prior to important events and great discoveries. Through the years the all-enveloping fog of mystery which surrounded our brain-injured children had gradually dispelled. We had also begun to see other facts for which we had not bargained. These were facts about well children. A logical connection had emerged between the brain-injured (and therefore neurologically dysorganized) child and the well (and therefore neurologically organized) child, where earlier there were only disconnected and disassociated facts about well children. That logical sequence, as it emerged, had pointed insistently to a path by which we might markedly change man himself—and for the better. Was the neurological organization displayed by an average child necessarily the end of the path?

Now with brain-injured children performing as well as, or better than, average children the possibility of the path extending farther could be fully seen.

It had always been assumed that neurological growth and its end product, ability, were a static and irrevocable fact: This child was capable and that child was not. This child was bright and that child was not.

Nothing could be further from the truth.

The fact is that neurological growth, which we had

always considered a static and irrevocable fact, is a dynamic and ever changing process.

In the severely brain-injured child we see the process of neurological growth totally halted.

In the "retarded" child we see this process of neurological growth considerably slowed. In the average child it takes place at an average rate, and in the superior child, at above-average speed. We had now come to realize that the brain-injured child, the average child and the superior child are not three different kinds of children but instead represent a continuum ranging from the extreme neurological dysorganization which severe brain injury creates, through the more moderate neurological dysorganization caused by mild or moderate brain injury, through the average amount of neurological organization which the average child demonstrates, to the high degree of neurological organization which a superior child invariably demonstrates.

In the severely brain-injured child we had succeeded in restarting this process which had come to a halt, and in the "retarded" child we had accelerated it.

It was now clear that this process of neurological growth could be *speeded* as well as delayed.

Having repeatedly brought brain-injured children from neurological dysorganization to neurological organization of an average or even superior level by employing the simple nonsurgical techniques which had been developed, there was every reason to believe that these same techniques could be used to increase the amount of neurological organization demonstrated by average children. One of these techniques is to teach very small brain-injured children to read.

Nowhere is the ability to raise neurological organization more clearly demonstrated than when you teach a well baby to read.

table of contents

a note to parents

Reading is one of the highest functions of the human brain—of all creatures on earth, only people can read.

Reading is one of the most important functions in life, since virtually all learning is based on the ability to read.

It is truly astonishing that it has taken us so many years to realize that the younger a child is when he learns to read, the easier it will be for him to read and the better he will read.

Children can read words when they are one year old, sentences when they are two, and whole books when they are three years old—and they love it.

The realization that they have this ability, and why they have it, took a long time.

Although we actually didn't begin to teach tiny children to read at The Institutes until 1961, the understanding of how the human brain functions (which was necessary to indicate the possibility that this could be done) had taken twenty years on the part of an entire team of various specialists to achieve.

This team of child developmentalists, physicians, educators, reading specialists, brain surgeons and psychologists had begun their work with brain-injured children and this led them to a many-year study of how the well child's brain develops. This in turn led to new and rather startling information about how children learn, what children learn—and what children *can* learn.

When the team had seen many brain-injured children read, and read well, at three years of age and younger, it became obvious that something was wrong with what was happening—to *well* children. This book is one of several results.

What this book says is precisely what we have been telling the parents of hurt kids and well kids since 1961. The results of telling them have been most gratifying both to the parents of the children and to us.

This book has been written at the insistence of these parents, who wanted what we have told them in book form for themselves and for other parents.

1
the facts and Tommy

I've been telling you he can read.

—MR. LUNSKI

It began spontaneously, this gentle revolution.

The strange thing about it is that it came about in the end by accident.

The kids, who *are* the gentle revolutionaries, didn't know that they would be able to read if the tools were given them, and the adults in the television industry, who finally furnished them, knew neither that the children had the ability nor that television would supply the tools which would bring about the gentle revolution.

The lack of tools is the reason it took so long for it to occur, but now that it's here, we parents must become conspirators in fostering this splendid revolution, not to make it less gentle but to make it more rapid so that the kids can reap its rewards.

It's astonishing really, that the secret has not been discovered by the kids long before this. It's a wonder that they, with all their brightness—because bright they are—didn't catch on.

The only reason some adult hasn't given the secret away to the two-year-olds is that we adults haven't known it either. Of course, if we had known, we would never have allowed it to remain a secret because it's far too important to the kids and to us too.

The trouble is that we have made the print too small.

The trouble is that we have made the print too small.

The trouble is that we have made the print too small.

The trouble is that we have made the print too small.

It is even possible to make the print too small for the sophisticated visual pathway—which includes the brain—of the adult to read.

It is almost impossible to make the print too big to read.

But it *is* possible to make it too small, and that's just what we've done.

The underdeveloped visual pathway, from the eye through the visual areas of the brain itself, of the one-, two- or three-year-old just can't differentiate one word from another.

But now, as we've said, television has given away the whole secret—through commercials. The result is that when the man on television says, *Gulf, Gulf, Gulf,* in a nice clear loud voice and the television screen shows the word **GULF** in nice big clear letters, the kids all learn to recognize the word—and they don't even know the alphabet.

For the truth is that tiny children can learn to read. It is safe to say that in particular very young children can read, *provided* that, in the beginning, you make the print very big.

But we know both of those things now.

Now that we know we have got to do something about it, because what will happen when we teach all the little kids to read will be very important to the world.

But isn't it easier for a child to understand a spoken word rather than a written one? Not at all. The child's brain, which is the only organ that has learning capacity, "hears" the clear loud television words through the ear and interprets them as only the brain can. Simultaneously the child's brain "sees" the big clear television words through his eye and interprets them in exactly the same manner.

It makes no difference to the brain whether it "sees" a sight or "hears" a sound. It can understand both equally well. All that is required is that the sounds be loud enough and clear enough for the ear to hear and the words big enough and clear enough for the eye to see so that the brain can interpret them—the former we have done but the latter we have failed to do.

People have probably always talked to children in a louder voice than they use with adults, and we still do so, instinctively realizing that children cannot hear and simultaneously understand normal adult conversational tones.

Nobody would think of talking to one-year-olds in a normal voice—we all virtually shout at them.

Try talking to a two-year-old in a conversational tone and chances are that he will neither hear nor understand you. It is likely that if his back is turned he will not even pay attention to you.

Even a three-year-old, if spoken to in a conversational tone, is unlikely to understand or even heed you if there are conflicting sounds or another conversation in the room.

Everyone talks loudly to children, and the younger the child is the louder we talk.

Suppose, for the sake of argument, that we adults had long ago decided to speak to each other in sounds just soft enough so that no child could hear and understand them. Suppose, however, that these sounds were just loud enough for his auditory pathway to have become sufficiently sophisticated to hear and understand soft sounds when he got to be six years of age.

Under this set of circumstances we would probably give children "hearing readiness" tests at six years of age. If we found that he could "hear" but not understand words (which would certainly be the case, since his auditory pathway could not distinguish soft sounds until now), it is possible that we would now introduce him to the spoken language by saying the letter A to him, and then B, and so on until he had learned the alphabet, before beginning to teach him how words sound.

One is led to conclude that perhaps there would be a great many children with a problem of "hearing" words and sentences, and perhaps a popular book called *Why Johnny Can't Hear*.

The above is precisely what we have done with written language. We have made it too small for the child to "see and understand" it.

Now let's make another supposition.

If we had spoken in whispers while simultaneously writing words and sentences very large and distinct, very young children would be able to read but would be unable to understand verbal language.

Now suppose that television were introduced with its big written words and with loud spoken words to go with them. Naturally all kids could read the words, but there would also be many children who would begin to understand the spoken word at the astonishing age of two or three.

And that, in reverse, is what is happening today in reading!

TV has also shown us several other interesting things about children.

The first is that youngsters watch most "kiddie programs" without paying constant attention; but as everyone knows, when the commercials come on the children run to the television set to *hear* about and *read* about what the products contain and what they are supposed to do.

The point here is not that television commercials are pitched to the two-year-old set, nor is it that gasoline or what it contains has any special fascination for two-year-olds, because it does not.

The truth is that the children can *learn* from commercials with the big enough, clear enough, loud enough, repeated message and that all children have a rage to learn.

Children would rather *learn* about something than simply be amused by a Happy Harry—and that's a fact.

As a result then, the kids ride down the road in the family car and blithely read the Esso sign, the

Gulf sign and the Coca-Cola sign as well as many others—and *that's* a fact.

There is no need to ask the question, "*Can* very small children learn to read?" They've answered that, they *can*. The question that should be asked is, "*What* do we want children to read?" Should we restrict their reading to the names of products and the rather strange chemicals which these products or our stomachs contain, or should we let them read something which might enrich their lives and which might be a part of Maplewood Avenue rather than Madison Avenue?

Let's look at all of the basic facts.

1. Tiny children *want* to learn to read.
2. Tiny children *can* learn to read.
3. Tiny children *are* learning to read.
4. Tiny children *should* learn to read.

I shall devote a chapter to each of these four facts. Each of them is true and each is simple. Perhaps that has been a large part of the problem. *There are few disguises harder to penetrate than the deceptive cloak of simplicity.*

It was probably this very simplicity that made it difficult for us to understand, or even to believe, the absurd story that Mr. Lunski told us about Tommy.

It's strange that it took us so long to pay any

attention to Mr. Lunski, because when we first saw Tommy at The Institutes we were already aware of all the things we needed to know in order to understand what was happening to Tommy.

Tommy was the fourth child in the Lunski family. The Lunski parents hadn't had much time for formal schooling and had worked very hard to support their three nice, normal children. By the time Tommy was born Mr. Lunski owned a taproom and things were looking up.

However, Tommy was born very severely brain-injured. When he was two years old he was admitted for neurosurgical examination at a fine hospital in New Jersey. The day Tommy was discharged the chief neurosurgeon had a frank talk with Mr. and Mrs. Lunski. The doctor explained that his studies had shown that Tommy was a vegetable-like child who would never walk or talk and should therefore be placed in an institution for life.

All of Mr. Lunski's determined Polish ancestry reinforced his American stubbornness as he stood up to his great height, hitched up his considerable girth and announced, "Doc, you're all mixed up. That's *our* kid."

The Lunskis spent many months searching for someone who would tell them that it didn't necessarily have to be that way. The answers were all the same.

By Tommy's third birthday, however, they had found Dr. Eugene Spitz, Chief of Neurosurgery at Children's Hospital in Philadelphia.

After carefully making his own neurosurgical studies, Dr. Spitz told the parents that while Tommy was indeed severely brain-injured, perhaps something might be done for him at a group of institutions in a suburb called Chestnut Hill.

Tommy arrived at The Institutes for the Achievement of Human Potential when he was just three years and two weeks old. He could not move or talk.

Tommy's brain injury and his resultant problems were evaluated at The Institutes. A treatment program was prescribed for Tommy which would reproduce the normal developmental growth of well children in Tommy. The parents were taught how to carry out this program at home and were told that if they adhered to it without failure, Tommy might be greatly improved. They were to return in sixty days for a re-evaluation, and if Tommy were improved, for program revisions.

There was no question but that the Lunskis would follow the strict program. They did so with religious intensity.

By the time they returned for the second visit, Tommy could creep.

Now the Lunskis attacked the program with energy inspired by success. So determined were they that when their car broke down on the way to Philadelphia for the third visit, they simply bought a used car and continued to their appointment. They could hardly wait to tell us that Tommy could now say his first two words—"Mommy" and "Daddy." Tommy was now three and a half and could creep on hands and knees. Then his mother tried something only a mother would try with a child like Tommy. In much the same manner that a father buys a football for his infant son, Mother bought an alphabet book for her three-and-a-half-year-old, severely brain-injured, two-word-speaking son. Tommy, she announced, was very bright, whether he could walk and talk or not. Anyone who had any sense could see it simply by looking in his eyes!

While our tests for intelligence in brain-injured children during those days were a good deal more involved than Mrs. Lunski's, they were no more accurate than hers. We agreed that Tommy was intelligent all right, but to teach a brain-injured three-and-a-half-year-old to read—well, that was another question.

We paid very little attention when Mrs. Lunski announced that Tommy, then four years of age, could read *all* of the *words* in the alphabet book even more easily than he could read the letters. We were more concerned and pleased with his speech, which was progressing constantly, as was his physical mobility.

By the time Tommy was four years and two months old his father announced that he could read all of a Dr. Seuss book called *Green Eggs and Ham*. We smiled politely and noted how remarkably Tommy's speech and movement were improving.

When Tommy was four years and six months old Mr. Lunski announced that Tommy could read, and had read, *all* of the Dr. Seuss books. We noted on the chart that Tommy was progressing beautifully, as well as the fact that Mr. Lunski "said" Tommy could read.

When Tommy arrived for his eleventh visit he had just had his fifth birthday. Although both Dr. Spitz and we were delighted with the superb advances Tommy was making, there was nothing to indicate at the beginning of the visit that this day would be an important one for all children. Nothing, that is, except Mr. Lunski's usual nonsensical report. Tommy, Mr. Lunski announced, could now read anything, including the *Reader's Digest*, and what was more, he could understand it, and what was more than that, he'd started doing it before his fifth birthday.

We were saved from the necessity of having to comment on this by the arrival of one of the kitchen staff with our lunch—tomato juice and a hamburger. Mr. Lunski, noting our lack of response, took a piece of paper from the desk and wrote, "Glenn Doman likes to drink tomato juice and eat hamburger."

Tommy, following his father's instructions, read this easily and with the proper accents and inflections. He did not hesitate as does the seven-year-old, reading each word separately without understanding of the sentence itself.

"Write another sentence," we said slowly.

Mr. Lunski wrote, "Tommy's daddy likes to drink beer and whiskey. He has a great big fat belly from drinking beer and whiskey at Tommy's Tavern."

Tommy had read only the first three words aloud when he began to laugh. The funny part about Dad's belly was down on the fourth line since Mr. Lunski was writing in large letters.

This severely brain-injured little child was actually reading much faster than he was reciting the words aloud at his normal speaking rate. Tommy was not only reading, he was speed-reading and his comprehension was obvious!

The fact that we were thunderstruck was written on our faces. We turned to Mr. Lunski.

"I've been telling you he can read," said Mr. Lunski.

After that day none of us would ever be the same, for this was the last piece of puzzle in a pattern which had been forming for more than twenty years.

Tommy had taught us that even a severely brain-injured child can learn to read far earlier than normal children usually do.

Tommy, of course, was immediately subjected to full-scale testing by a group of experts who were brought from Washington for this purpose within a week. Tommy—severely brain-injured and just barely five years old—could read better than the average child twice his age—and with complete comprehension.

By the time Tommy was six he walked, although this was relatively new to him and he was still a little shaky; he read at the sixth-grade level (eleven-to-twelve-year-old level). Tommy was not going to spend his life in an institution, but his parents were looking for a "special" school to put Tommy in come the following September. Special *high*, that is, not special low. Fortunately there are a few experimental schools now for exceptional "gifted" children. Tommy has had the dubious "gift" of severe brain injury and the unquestionable gift of parents who love him very much indeed and who believed that at least one kid wasn't achieving his potential.

Tommy, in the end, was a catalyst for twenty years of study. Maybe it would be more accurate to say he was a fuse for an explosive charge that had been growing in force for twenty years.

The fascinating thing was that Tommy *wanted* very much to read and enjoyed it tremendously.

2

tiny children
want to learn
to read

*It has me beaten, we haven't been able to
stop her reading since she was three.*

—MRS. GILCHRIST,
MOTHER OF FOUR-YEAR-OLD MARY,
Newsweek (MAY 13, 1963)

There has never been, in the history of man, an
adult scientist who has been half so curious as is
any child between the ages of eighteen months and
four years. We adults have mistaken this superb
curiosity about everything as a lack of ability to
concentrate.

We have of course observed our children carefully, but we have not always understood what
their actions mean. For one thing, many people

often use two very different words as if they were the same. The words are *learn* and *educate*.

The *American College Dictionary* tells us that *learn* means: 1. To acquire knowledge of or skill in by study, instruction, or experience . . ."

To *educate* means: "1. To develop the faculties and powers of by teaching, instruction, or schooling . . . and 2. To provide education for; send to school . . ."

In other words, learning generally refers to the process that goes on in the one who is acquiring knowledge, while educating is often the learning process guided by a teacher or school. Although everyone really knows this, these two processes are frequently thought of as one and the same.

Because of this we sometimes feel that since formal *education* begins at six years of age, the more important processes of learning also begin at six years of age.

Nothing could be further from the truth.

The truth is that a child begins to learn just after birth. By the time he is six years of age and begins his schooling he has already absorbed a fantastic amount of information, fact for fact, perhaps more than he will learn the rest of his life.

By the time a child is six he has learned most of the basic facts about himself and his family. He has learned about his neighbors and his relationships to them, his world and his relationship to

it, and a host of other facts which are literally un-
countable. Most significantly, he has learned at
least one whole language and sometimes more
than one. (The chances are very small that he will
ever truly master an additional language after
he is six.)

All this before he has seen the inside of a
classroom.

The process of learning through these years pro-
ceeds at great speed unless we thwart it. If we
appreciate and encourage it, the process will take
place at a truly unbelievable rate.

A tiny child has, burning within him, a boundless desire to learn.

We can kill this desire entirely only by destroying him completely.

We can come close to quenching it by isolating
him. We read occasionally of, say, a thirteen-year-
old idiot who is found in an attic chained to a bedpost, presumably because he was an idiot. The
reverse is probably the case. It is extremely likely
that he is an idiot because he was chained to the
bedpost. To appreciate this fact we must realize
that only psychotic parents would chain any child.
A parent chains a child to a bedpost *because* the
parent is psychotic, and the result is an idiot child
because he has been denied virtually all opportunity
to learn.

We can *diminish* the child's desire to *learn* by

limiting the experiences to which we expose him. Unhappily we have done this almost universally by drastically underestimating what he can learn.

We can *increase* his learning markedly, simply by removing many of the physical restrictions we have placed upon him.

We can *multiply* by many times the knowledge he absorbs and even his potential if we appreciate his superb capacity for learning and give him unlimited opportunity while simultaneously encouraging him to do so.

Throughout history there have been isolated but numerous cases of people who have actually taught tiny children to read, and do other advanced things, by appreciating and encouraging them. In *all* of the cases which we were able to find, the results of such preplanned home opportunity for children to learn ranged from "excellent" to "astonishing" in producing happy, well-adjusted children with exceptionally high intelligence.

It is very important to bear in mind that these children had *not* been found to have high intelligence first and then been given unusual opportunities to learn, but instead were simply children whose parents decided to expose them to as much information as possible at a very early age.

Throughout history the great teachers have pointed out again and again that we must foster a love of learning in our children. Unhappily they have not told us often enough how we might do this. The ancient Hebrew scholars taught parents to bake cakes in the form of the letters of the Hebrew alphabet which the child had to identify before he was allowed to eat the cake. In a similar way, Hebrew words were written with honey on the child's slate. The child would then read the words and lick them off so that "the words of the law might be sweet on his lips."

Once an adult who cares about children is made sensitive to what a young child is really doing, he wonders how he could ever have missed it in the first place.

Look carefully at the eighteen-month-old child and see what he does.

In the first place he drives everybody to distraction.

Why does he? Because he won't stop being curious. He cannot be dissuaded, disciplined or confined out of this desire to learn, no matter how hard we try—and we have certainly tried very hard.

He wants to learn about the lamp and the coffee cup and the electric light socket and the newspaper and everything else in the room—which means that he knocks over the lamp, spills the coffee cup, puts his finger in the electric light socket and tears up the newspaper. He is learning constantly and, quite naturally, we can't stand it.

From the way he carries on we have concluded that he is hyperactive and unable to pay attention, when the simple truth is that he pays attention to everything. He is superbly alert in every way he can be to learn about the world. He sees, hears, feels, smells and tastes. There is no other way to learn except by these five routes into the brain, and the child uses them all.

He sees the lamp and therefore pulls it down so that he can feel it, hear it, look at it, smell it and taste it. Given the opportunity, he will do all these things to the lamp—and he will do the same to every object in the room. He will not demand to be let out of the room until he has absorbed all he can, through every sense available to him, about every object in the room. He is doing his best to learn and, of course, we are doing our best to stop him because his learning process is far too expensive.

We parents have devised several methods of coping with the curiosity of the very young child and, unfortunately, almost all of them are at the expense of the child's learning.

The first general method is the give-him-something-to-play-with-that-he-can't-break school of thought. This usually means a nice pink rattle to play with. It may even be a more complicated toy than a rattle, but it's still a toy. Presented with such an object the child promptly looks at it (which is why toys have bright colors), bangs it to find out if it makes a noise (which is why rattles rattle), feels it (which is why toys don't have sharp edges), tastes it (which is why the paint is non-poisonous) and even smells it (we have not yet figured out how toys ought to smell, which is why they don't smell at all). This process takes about ninety seconds.

Now that he knows all he wants to know about the toy for the present, the child promptly abandons it and turns his attention to the box in which it came. The child finds the box just as interesting as the toy—which is why we should always buy toys that come in boxes—and learns all about the box. This also takes about ninety seconds. In fact, the child will frequently pay more attention to the box than to the toy itself. Because he is allowed to break the box, he may be able to learn how it is made. This is an advantage he does not have with the toy itself, since we make toys unbreakable, which of course reduces his ability to learn.

Therefore it would seem that buying a child a toy that comes in a box would be a good way to double his attention span. But have we—or have we merely given him twice as much interesting material? It is quite clear that the latter is the case. In short, we must conclude that a child's attention span is related to the amount of material he has available to learn about rather than believing, as we often do, that a child is incapable of paying attention for very long.

If you simply watch children, you will see dozens of examples of this. Yet, despite all of the evidence that our eyes give us, we too often come to the conclusion that when a child has a short attention span, he just isn't very smart. This deduction insidiously implies that he (like all other children) is not very bright because he is very young. One wonders what our conclusions would be if the two-year-old sat in a corner and quietly played with the rattle for five hours. Probably the parents of such a child would be even more upset—and with good reason.

The second general method of coping with his attempts to learn is the put-him-back-in-the-play-pen school of thought.

The only proper thing about the play pen is its name—it is truly a pen. We should at least be honest about such devices and stop saying, "Let's go buy a play pen for the baby." Let's tell the truth and admit that we buy them for ourselves.

There is a cartoon which shows Mother sitting in a play pen, reading and smiling contentedly while the children play outside the pen, unable to get at her. This cartoon, aside from its humorous element, also suggests another truth: The mother who already knows about the world can afford to be isolated, while the children outside, who have much to learn, can continue their explorations.

Few parents realize what a play pen really costs. Not only does the play pen restrict the child's ability to learn about the world, which is fairly obvious, but it seriously restricts his neurological growth by limiting his ability to crawl and creep (processes vital to normal growth). This in turn inhibits the development of his vision, manual competence, hand-eye coördination, and a host of other things.

We parents have persuaded ourselves that we are buying the play pen to protect the child from hurting himself by chewing on an electric cord or falling down the stairs. Actually we are penning him up so that *we* do not have to make sure he is safe. In terms of our time we are being penny-wise and pound-foolish.

How much more sensible it would be, if we must have a play pen, to use one which is twelve feet long and twenty-four inches wide so that the baby may crawl, creep and learn during these vital years of his life. With such a play pen the child can move twelve feet by crawling or creeping in a straight line before he finds himself against the bars at the opposite end. Such a play pen is infinitely more convenient to parents also, since it only takes up space along one wall rather than filling up the room.

The play pen as an implement to prevent learning is unfortunately much more effective than the rattle, because after the child has spent ninety seconds learning about each toy Mother puts in (which is why he will throw each of them out as he finishes learning about it), he is then stuck.

Thus we have succeeded in preventing him from destroying things (one way of learning) by physically confining him. This approach, which puts the child in a physical, emotional and educational vacuum, will not fail so long as we can stand his anguished screams to get out; or, assuming that we can stand it, until he's big enough to climb out and renew his search for learning.

Does all the above assume that we are in favor of the child breaking the lamp? Not at all. It assumes only that we have had far too little respect for the small child's desire to learn, despite all the clear indications he gives us *that he wants desperately to learn everything he can, and as quickly as possible.*

Apocryphal stories keep creeping up which, even if they are not true, are revealing nevertheless.

There is the story of the two five-year-old kindergarten boys standing in the schoolyard when a plane flashes by overhead. One youngster says that the airplane is supersonic. The other refutes this on the basis that the wings are not swept back enough. The recess bell interrupts the discussion and the first child says, "We've got to stop now and go back to stringing those damned beads."

The story is overdrawn, but true in implication.

Consider the three-year-old who asks, "Daddy, why is the sun hot?" "How did the little man get into the TV set?" "What makes the flowers grow, Mommy?"

While the child is displaying an electronic, astronomical and biological curiosity, we too often tell him to run along and play with his toys. Simultaneously we may well be concluding that because he is very young he wouldn't understand and, besides, that he has a very short attention span. He certainly has—for most toys, at least.

We have succeeded in keeping our children carefully isolated from learning in a period of life when the desire to learn is at its peak.

The human brain is unique in that it is the only container of which it can be said that the more you put into it, the more it will hold.

Between nine months and four years the ability to absorb information is unparalleled, and the desire to do so is higher than it will ever be again. Yet during this period we keep the child clean, well fed, safe from the world about him—and in a learning vacuum.

It is ironic that when the child is older we will

tell him repeatedly how foolish he is for not want-ing to learn about astronomy, physics and biology. Learning, we will tell him, is the most important thing in life, and indeed it is.

We have, however, overlooked the other side of the coin.

Learning is also the greatest game in life, and the most fun.

We have assumed that children hate to learn essentially because most children have disliked or even despised school. Again we have mistaken schooling for learning. Not all children in school are learning—just as not all children who are learning are doing so in school.

My own experiences in first grade were perhaps typical of what they have been for centuries. In general the teacher told us to sit down, keep quiet, look at her and listen to her while she began a process called teaching which, she said, would be mutually painful but from which we would learn—or else.

In my own case, that first-grade teacher's prophecy proved to be correct; it was painful and, at least for the first twelve years, I hated every minute of it. I'm sure it was not a unique experi-ence.

The process of learning should be fun of the highest order, for it is indeed the greatest game in life. Sooner or later all bright people come to this conclusion. Time and again you hear people say, "It was a great day. I learned a great many things I didn't know before." One even hears, "I had a terrible day *but* I learned something."

A recent experience, which climaxed hundreds of similar but less amusing situations, serves as an excellent example of the fact that tiny children want to learn to the degree that they are unable to distinguish learning from fun. They keep this attitude until we adults convince them that learning is *not* fun.

Our team had been seeing a brain-injured three-year-old child for a number of months and she had reached the point where it was time to introduce her to reading. It was important to this child's rehabilitation that she learn to read, because it is impossible to inhibit a single human brain function without to some degree suppressing the total sum of brain function. Conversely, if we teach a very young brain-injured child to read we will assist materially in his speech and other functions. It was for this reason that we had prescribed that this child be taught to read upon this particular visit.

The child's father was, understandably, skeptical about teaching his brain-injured three-year-old daughter to read. He was persuaded to do so only because of the splendid physical and speech progress that the child had made up to this time.

When he returned for a progress check two months later, he gleefully told the following story: While he had agreed to do as he had been instructed, he did not believe that it would work. He had also decided that if he was going to try to teach his brain-injured child to read, he was going to do it in what he considered to be a "typical classroom environment."

He had, therefore, built a schoolroom, complete with blackboard and desks, in his basement. He had then invited his well seven-year-old daughter to attend also.

Predictably, the seven-year-old had taken one look at the classroom and yelped with joy. She had the biggest toy in the whole neighborhood. Bigger than a baby carriage, bigger than a doll house. She had her own private school.

In July the seven-year-old went out into the neighborhood and recruited five children, ranging from three to five years of age, to "play school."

Of course, they were excited by the idea and agreed to be good children so they could go to school like their older brothers and sisters. They played school five days a week all summer long. The seven-year-old was the teacher and the smaller children were her pupils.

The children were not forced to play this game. It was simply the best game they had ever found to play.

The "school" closed down in September when the seven-year-old teacher went back to her own second grade.

As a result, in that particular neighborhood there are now five children, ranging in age from three to five years, who can read. They can't read Shakespeare, but they can read the twenty-five words that the seven-year-old teacher taught them. They read them and they understand them.

Surely this seven-year-old must be listed among the most accomplished educators in history—or else we must conclude that three-year-olds *want* to read.

We choose to believe that it is the three-year-old's desire to read rather than the seven-year-old's teaching skill which makes for learning.

Finally it is important to note that when a three-year-old is taught to read a book, he can pay attention to the book for long periods of time, appears to be very bright, and stops smashing lamps altogether; but he is still only three years old and still finds most toys to be of interest for about ninety seconds.

While, naturally, no child wants specifically to learn to read until he knows that reading exists, all children want to absorb information about everything around them, and under the proper circumstances reading is one of these things.

3
tiny children
can learn
to read

One day not long ago I found her on the living-room floor thumbing through a French book. She simply told me, "Well, Mummy, I've read all the English books in the house."

—MRS. GILCHRIST,
Newsweek (MAY 13, 1963)

Very young children can and do learn to read words, sentences and paragraphs in exactly the same way they learn to understand spoken words, sentences and paragraphs.

Again the facts are simple—beautiful but simple. We have already stated that the eye sees but does not understand what is seen and that the ear hears but does not understand what is heard. Only the brain understands.

When the ear apprehends, or picks up, a spoken word or message, this auditory message is broken down into a series of electrochemical impulses and flashed to the unhearing brain, which then reassembles and *comprehends* in terms of the meaning the word was intended to convey.

In precisely the same manner it happens that when the eye apprehends a printed word or message, this visual message is broken down into a series of electrochemical impulses and flashed to the unseeing brain to be reassembled and comprehended as reading.

It is a magical instrument, the brain.

Both the visual pathway and the auditory pathway travel through the brain where *both* messages are interpreted by the same brain process.

Visual *acuity* and auditory *acuity* actually have very little to do with it, unless they are very poor indeed.

There are many animals that see or hear better than any human being. Nonetheless, no chimpanzee, no matter how acute his vision or hearing, will ever read the word "freedom" through his eye or understand it through his ear. He hasn't the brain for it.

To begin understanding the human brain we must consider the instant of conception rather than the moment of birth, because the superb and very little understood process of brain growth begins at conception.

From conception on, the human brain grows at an explosive rate which is continually on a descending scale.

Explosive and *descending*.

The whole process is essentially complete at the age of eight.

At conception the fertile egg is microscopic in size. Twelve days later the embryo is large enough so that the brain can be differentiated. This is long before Mother knows she is pregnant, so phenomenally fast is the rate of growth.

While the *rate* of growth is fantastic, this rate is always slower than the day before.

By birth the child weighs six or seven pounds, which is millions of times what the egg weighed nine months earlier at conception. It is obvious that if his *rate* of growth were the same in the next nine months as it was in the previous nine months, he would weigh thousands of tons when he was nine months old and many millions of tons when he was eighteen months old.

The process of brain growth matches the body growth but is on an even more descending rate. This can be seen clearly when one appreciates the fact that at birth the child's brain makes up 11 per cent of the total body weight, while in adults it's only 2.5 per cent.

When the child is five the growth of the brain is 80 per cent complete.

When he is eight the process of brain growth is, as we have said, virtually complete.

During the years between eight and eighty we have less brain growth than we had in the single year (and slowest of the first eight years) between the ages of seven and eight.

In addition to this basic understanding of how the brain grows, it is important to understand which of its functions are most important to humans.

There are just six neurological functions which are exclusive to man, and these six functions characterize man and set him apart from other creatures.

These are the six functions of a layer of the brain known as the *human* cortex. These exclusively human abilities are present and functioning by eight years of age. They are worth knowing.

1. Only man is able to walk entirely upright.
2. Only man speaks in abstract, symbolic, devised language.
3. Only man is able to combine his unique manual competence with motor abilities listed above to write his language.

The first three skills listed are of a *motor* nature (expressive) and are based upon the remaining three, which are *sensory* in nature (receptive).

4. Only man understands the abstract, symbolic, devised language which he hears.

5. Only man can identify an object by touch alone.

6. Only man sees in a manner which enables him to read the abstract language when it is in written form.

An eight-year-old child is capable of all of these functions since he walks, talks, writes, reads, understands spoken language and identifies objects by touch at that age. It is evident that from that time on we are simply talking about a sort of lateral multiplication of these six exclusively human abilities, rather than the addition of new oncs.

Since all of man's later life is, to a large degree, dependent upon these six functions, which are developed in the first eight years of life, an investigation and description of the various phases which exist during that molding period of life is very important.

THE PERIOD FROM BIRTH TO ONE

This period of life is *vital* to the child's whole future.

It is true that we keep him warm, fed and clean, but we also seriously restrict his neurological growth.

What *should* happen to him during this time could easily be the subject of a whole book. Suffice it to say here that during this period of life the infant should have almost unlimited opportunity for movement, for physical exploration and for experience. Our present society and culture usually deny him this. Such opportunity, on the rare occasions when it is afforded a child, results in physically and neurologically superior children. *What the adult will be in terms of physical and neurological ability is determined more strongly in this period than in any other.*

THE PERIOD FROM ONE TO FIVE

This period of life is *crucial* to the child's whole future.

During this period of life we love him, make sure he doesn't hurt himself, smother him with toys and send him to nursery school. And, totally unaware, we are doing our best to prevent learning.

What *should* happen to him during these crucial years is that we should be satisfying his staggering thirst for raw material, which he wants to soak up in all possible forms but particularly in terms of language, whether spoken and heard or printed and read.

It is during this period of life that the child should learn to read, thus unlocking the door to the golden treasury of all things written by man in history, the sum of man's knowledge.

It is during these not-to-be-relived years, these years of insatiable curiosity, that the child's whole intellectual being will be established. What the child can be, what his interests will be, what his capacities will be, are being determined in these years. An unlimited number of factors will bear on him as an adult. Friends, society and culture may influence what job he will do in life, and some of these factors may be harmful to his full potential.

While such circumstances of adult life may combine to lower his capacity to enjoy life and to be productive, he will not rise above the potential that is established during this crucial period of his life. It is for this all-important reason that every opportunity should be given the child to gain knowledge, which he enjoys beyond all other things.

It is ridiculous to assume that when a child's insatiable curiosity is being satisfied, and in a manner which he adores, we are depriving him of his precious childhood. Such an attitude would be completely unworthy of mention, were it not so frequently encountered. One rarely finds parents, however, who believe that there is any loss of "precious childhood" when they see the eagerness with which a child engages himself in reading a book with Mommy, as compared to his anguished screams to get out of the play pen or his total boredom in the midst of a mountain of toys.

Learning during this period of life is, moreover, a compelling necessity and we are thwarting all of nature when we try to prevent it. *It is necessary for survival.*

The kitten that "plays" by leaping upon the ball of wool is simply using the wool as a substitute for a mouse. The puppy that "plays" in mock ferocity with other puppies is learning how to survive when attacked.

Survival in the human world is dependent upon the ability to communicate, and language is the tool of communication.

The child's play, like the kitten's play, is purposeful and aimed at learning rather than amusement.

The acquisition of language in all of its forms is one of the prime purposes for the child's play. We must be careful to see it for what it is rather than assume that such play is geared toward amusement.

The need to learn during this period of life is, for the child, a stark necessity. Isn't it wonderful that an omniscient Nature made the child also love learning? Isn't it awful that we have so terribly misunderstood what a child is, and placed so many roadblocks in Nature's way?

This then is the period of life in which the child's brain is an open door to all information. During this period of life he takes in all information without conscious effort of any sort. This is the period of life in which he can learn to read easily and naturally. He should be given the opportunity to do so.

It is during this period that he can learn to speak a foreign language, even as many as five, which he at present fails to learn through high school and college. They should be offered to him. He will learn easily now, but with great difficulty later.

It is during this period that he should be exposed to all the basic information about written language, which he now learns with much effort between the ages of six and ten. He will learn it more quickly and easily.

It is more than a unique opportunity, it is a sacred duty. We must open the floodgate of all basic knowledge to him.

We shall never again have an equal opportunity.

THE PERIOD FROM FIVE TO EIGHT

This period of life is *very important* to the child's whole life.

During this important time, which is virtually the end of his plastic, pliable, formative days, he begins school. What a traumatic period of life this can be! What reader does not remember this part of his life, no matter how long ago it may have been? The experience of entering kindergarten and the two years that follow are frequently the earliest memory that an adult retains. Often it is not remembered with pleasure.

Why should this be, when children want so desperately to learn? Can we interpret this to mean that a child does not want to learn? Or is it more likely that this indicates we are making some very basic and important mistake?

If we are making such a basic mistake, what could it be? Consider the facts in the case.

We are suddenly taking this child who, up until now, has probably spent little, if any, time away from home, and introduce him to an entirely new physical and social world. It would be an indictment of his happiness in the home situation if the five- or six-year-old did not miss home and Mother during this very important formative period of life. Simultaneously we begin to introduce him to group discipline and early education.

We must remember that the child is long on the ability to learn but still very short on judgment. The result is that the child associates the unhappiness of being suddenly away from Mother with the early educational experience, and thus from the beginning the child associates learning with what is, at best, a vague unhappiness. This is hardly a fine beginning for the most important job in life.

By doing this we have also dealt the teacher a severe blow. It is little wonder that many teachers face their task with grim determination rather than with joyous anticipation. She has two strikes against her when first she lays eyes on her new pupil.

How much better it would be for pupil, teacher and the world if, by that first day of school, the new pupil had already acquired and kept a love of the joy of learning.

If this were the case, the child's love of reading and learning, which was now about to be increased, would go a very long way toward minimizing the psychological blow of having Mommy's apron strings cut.

In fact, in the relatively isolated cases where the child is introduced to learning at a very young age, it is gratifying to watch the child's love of learning become a love of school as well. It is significant that when these children do not feel well, they frequently attempt to conceal it from Mother (usually without success) so that they will not be kept home from school. What a delightful switch on our own childhood experiences when we frequently pretended illness (usually without success) in order *not* to have to go to school.

Our lack of recognition of these basic factors have led us to some very bad psychological actions. From an educational standpoint the seven-year-old is beginning to learn to read—but to read *about* trivia far below his interest, knowledge and ability.

What *should* be happening to the child during this important period of life between five and eight (assuming that the proper things had happened to him in the previous periods) is that he should be enjoying the material which would normally be presented to him when he is between eight and fourteen years of age.

That the results of this on a broad scale can only be good is evident, unless we are willing to accept the premise that ignorance leads to good and knowledge to evil; and that playing with a toy must result in happiness, while learning about language and the world means unhappiness.

It would be as silly to assume that filling the brain with information would somehow use it up, while keeping it empty would preserve it.

A person whose brain is loaded with useful information which he can use easily could be rated a genius, while a person whose brain is empty of information is called an idiot.

How much children will be able to learn under this new set of circumstances and how joyously they will learn it can only be the subject of our dreams until such time as large numbers of children have had this new opportunity. There is no doubt that the impact of these advanced children on the world can only be for the better.

The amount of knowledge we have prevented our children from gaining, measures our lack of appreciation for his genius to learn. How much they have succeeded in learning *despite* our prevention is a tribute to that same genius for absorbing information.

The newborn child is almost an exact duplicate of an empty electronic computer, although superior to such a computer in almost every way.

An empty computer is capable of receiving a vast amount of information readily and without effort.

So is a tiny child.

A computer is able to classify and file such information.

So is a child.

A computer is able to place such information in either permanent or temporary storage.

So is a child.

You can't expect a computer to give you accurate answers until you have put in the basic information upon which the question you ask is based. The computer cannot.

Neither can a child.

When you have placed sufficient basic information in the computer you will receive correct answers and even judgments from the machine.

So can you from a child.

The machine will accept all information you place in it, whether such information is correct or not.

So will a child.

The machine will reject no information which is put in in the proper form.

Neither will a child.

If incorrect information is put into the machine, future answers based upon this material will be incorrect.

So will the child's.

Here the parallel ends.

If incorrect information is placed in the computer, the machine can be emptied and reprogrammed.

This is not true of a child. The basic information placed in the child's brain for permanent storage has two limitations. The first limitation is that if you put misinformation into his brain during the first eight years of life, it is extremely difficult to erase it. The second limitation is that after he is eight years of age, he will absorb new material slowly and with greater difficulty.

Consider the Brooklyn child who says "pernt"

for "point," the Georgia child who says "heah" for "here," or the Massachusetts child who says "idear" for "idea." Very rarely does travel or education eliminate the local mispronunciation, which is in fact what all accents are, charming as they may sound. Even if later education places a sophisticated veneer over the basic learning of the first eight years, a period of great stress will wash it away.

The story is told of a beautiful but uneducated showgirl who married a wealthy man. He went to great lengths to educate his new wife and apparently was successful. But some years later while descending from a carriage in a manner befitting the cultured lady she had become, a priceless string of pearls became entangled in the carriage and broke, scattering the perfect pearls in all directions.

"Bejeesus," she is reported to have shouted, "me beads!"

What is placed in the child's brain during the first eight years of life is probably there to stay. We should, therefore, make every effort to make certain it is good and correct. It has been said, "Give me a child for the first eight years of life and you can do with him what you will thereafter." Nothing could be more true.

Everyone knows the ease with which small children memorize material, even material which they don't really understand.

Recently we saw an eight-year-old reading in a kitchen in which a dog was barking, a radio was playing, and in which a family argument was reaching a crescendo. The child was memorizing a poem of some length, to be recited in school the next day. He succeeded.

If an adult were asked to learn a poem today to recite before a group tomorrow, chances are that he would be panic-stricken. Supposing that he succeeded in doing so and that six months later he were asked to recite it again. The odds are great that he would be unable to do so, but that he would still remember poems he had recited as a child.

While a child is able to absorb and retain virtually all material presented to him during these vastly important years, his ability to learn the language is particularly unique, and it matters little if this language is spoken, which he learns in an auditory way, or written, which he learns in a visual way.

As has been pointed out, with every passing day the child's ability to take in information without effort *descends,* but it is also true that with each passing day his ability to make judgment goes up. Eventually that downward curve and the upward curve cross each other.

Prior to the time when the curves meet, the child is in some ways actually *superior* to the adult. The ability to learn languages is one of them.

Let's consider this unique factor of superiority in language acquisition.

The author spent four years trying to learn French as an adolescent and young adult and has twice been in France, but it is perfectly safe to say that he speaks virtually no French. Yet every normal French child and a good many below-average ones, even some mentally retarded, learn to speak French well, using all the basic rules of grammar, before they are six years old.

It's sort of upsetting when you think about it.

At first glance one might suspect that the difference is not in the child versus the adult, but instead in the fact that the child was in France while the adult was not, and thus exposed to hearing French all of the time and from every side.

Let's see if that is really the difference or whether the difference lies in the child's unlimited capacity and the adult's great difficulty to learn languages.

Literally tens of thousands of American Army officers have been assigned to foreign countries and many have tried to pick up the new language. Let's take the example of Major John Smith. Major Smith is thirty years of age and a fine physical specimen. He is also a college graduate and has an I.Q. at least fifteen points above average. Major Smith is assigned to a post in Germany.

Major Smith is sent to a German-language school, which he attends three nights a week. The Army language schools are fine institutions for adults, teaching by a system of spoken language and employing the best teachers available.

Major Smith works very hard to learn German, since it is important to his career and since he deals with German-speaking people as well as English-speaking people all day long.

Be all that as it may, a year later when he goes shopping with his five-year-old son, the child does most of the talking for the simple reason that he speaks fairly good German and Major Smith does not.

How can this be?

Dad has been taught German by the best German teacher that the Army can find, and yet, he does not really speak German, while his five-year-old child does!

Who taught the child? Nobody, really. It is just that he was at home during the day with the German-speaking maid. Who taught the maid German? Nobody, really.

Dad was taught German and doesn't speak it.

The child was not taught German and does speak it.

Lest the reader be sucked into the trap of still believing that the difference lies in the slightly different environments of Major Smith and his son rather than in the child's unique ability and the adult's relative inability to learn languages, let us quickly consider the case of *Mrs.* Smith who has lived in the same house with the same maid as the child. Mrs. Smith has learned no more German than has Major Smith and far, far less than her son.

If our misuse of this unique ability to learn languages in childhood were not so sad and wasteful, it would be downright amusing.

If the Smiths happen to have a number of children when they go to Germany, the language proficiency will be directly inverse to the age of the family member.

The three-year-old, if there is one, will learn the most German.

The five-year-old will learn a great deal, but not as much as the three-year-old.

The ten-year-old will learn much German, but less than the five-year-old.

The fifteen-year-old will learn some German, which he will soon forget.

Poor Major and Mrs. Smith will actually learn almost no German at all.

The example which has been given, far from being an isolated case, is almost universally true. We have known children who have learned French or Spanish or German or Japanese or Iranian under these precise circumstances.

Another point we should like to make is not so much the child's innate ability to learn languages as it is the adult's *inability* to learn foreign tongues.

One is horrified when one considers the many millions of dollars that are wasted annually in high schools and colleges in the United States in trying vainly to teach languages to young adults who are almost incapable of learning them.

Let the reader consider if he or she *really* learned a foreign language in high school or in college.

If after four years of school-French the reader was able to struggle through asking a waiter in France for a glass of water, let him try to explain that he wants a glass of *iced* water. This is enough to convince all but the most hardy that four years of French wasn't enough. It's more than enough for any small child.

There is simply no question of the fact that a child, far from being an inferior, small-size adult, is in fact in many ways superior to grownups and that not the least of these ways is his almost uncanny faculty to absorb languages.

We have accepted almost without thought this truly miraculous ability.

Every normal child (and as has been said, a good many sub-normal ones) learns virtually an entire language between the age of one and five. He learns it with the exact accent of his nation, his state, his city, his neighborhood and his family. He learns it without visible effort and precisely as it is spoken. Who ever does this again?

Nor does it stop there.

Every child who is raised in a bilingual household will learn *two* languages before he is six years old. Moreover, he will learn the foreign language with the exact accent of the locale in which the parents learned it.

If an American child with Italian parents talks to a true Italian in later life, the Italian will say, "Ah, you are from Milan"—if that's where the parents were reared—"I can tell by your accent." This despite the fact that the Italian-American has never been outside the United States.

Every child who is raised in a trilingual household will speak three foreign languages before he is six years old, and so on.

The author recently had the experience, while in Brazil, of meeting a nine-year-old boy of average intelligence, who could understand, read and write nine languages rather fluently. Avi Roxannes was born in Cairo (French, Arabic and English) and his (Turkish) grandfather lived with them. When he was four the family moved to Israel where Avi's (Spanish) grandmother on his father's side joined them. In Israel he learned three more languages (Hebrew, German and Yiddish) and then at six years of age he moved to Brazil (Portuguese).

Since between them the parents speak as many languages as Avi does (but not individually), the Roxannes wisely carry on conversations with him in each of his nine tongues (individually where only one parent speaks a particular language, and collectively where they both do). Avi's parents are a good deal better linguists than most adults, having learned five languages each as children, but of course they are no match at all for Avi when it comes to English or Portuguese, which they learned as adults.

We have previously noted that there have been, in history, many carefully documented cases of what happened when parents have decided to teach very young children to do things which were—and still are—considered extraordinary.

One of these is the case of little Winifred, whose mother, Winifred Sackville Stoner, wrote a book about Winifred called *Natural Education,* which was published in 1914.

This mother began to encourage her child and to give her special opportunities to learn right after birth. We shall discuss the results of this attitude on Winifred's reading later in this book.

For now let's see what Mrs. Stoner had to say about her baby's ability with spoken language at five years of age:

"As soon as Winifred could make all her wants known I began to teach her Spanish through conversation and the same direct methods I had used in teaching English. I chose Spanish as her secondary tongue because it is the simplest of European languages. By the time that Winifred reached her fifth milestone she was able to express her thoughts in eight languages, and I have no doubt she could have doubled the number by this time if I had continued our game of word construction in various languages. But at this time I began to think that Esperanto would soon become the international medium of communication, and outside of developing linguistic ability a knowledge of many, many tongues could be of no great benefit to my little girl."

Later Mrs. Stoner says, "The usual methods of teaching languages in school through grammatical rules and transactions have proved an utter failure as regards the ability of pupils to use language as tools for thought expression.

"There are Latin professors who have taught Latin for half a century and do not really know colloquial Latin. When my little daughter was four years old she lost faith in the wisdom of some Latin professors when talking with a Latin instructor who did not understand the salutation '*Quid agis*' and gazed at her blankly when she spoke of the courses at the table '*ab ovo usque ad mala.*' "

Keeping in mind the child's remarkable ability to learn spoken language, let us stress again the fact that the process by which spoken language and written language is understood is precisely the same.

Then doesn't it follow that young children should also have a unique ability to read language? The fact is that, given an opportunity to do so, they do demonstrate such an ability. We shall shortly see some examples of this.

When a person or group is led by research to what appears to be a new and important idea, several things are necessary before duty compels that group to the publication and dissemination of this idea.

First the idea must be tested in life to see what the results of this idea being put into effect may be. They may be good or they may be bad or they may be indifferent.

Secondly, no matter how new such concepts may appear to be, it is possible that someone somewhere has had such ideas before and has used them. It is possible that they have somewhere reported their findings.

It is not only the privilege but, indeed, it is the

duty of people expressing such ideas to conduct a careful search of all available documents to determine what anyone else may have had to say on the subject. This is true even when it would appear to be an entirely new idea.

In the years between 1959 and 1962 our team was aware that other people were working with young children in the area of reading, both in and outside of the United States. We had a general idea of what they were doing and saying. While we agreed with much of what was being done and certainly that it was a good thing to do, we believed that the basis of such learning was neurological rather than psychological, emotional or educational.

When we began to study the literature on the subject intensively we were impressed by four facts:

1. The history of teaching little children to read was not new and indeed stretches back for centuries.
2. Often people generations apart do the same things although for different reasons and different philosophies.
3. Those who had decided to teach young children to read had all used systems which, although they varied somewhat in technique, had many common factors.

4. *Most importantly, in all of the cases we were able to find where small children were taught to read in the home, everyone who tried had succeeded, no matter what the method.*

Many of the cases were carefully observed and recorded in detail. Few were clearer than the aforementioned case of little Winifred. Mrs. Stoner had come to almost the same conclusions about early reading as those of us at The Institutes, although she did so without the neurological knowledge available to us.

Half a century ago, Mrs. Stoner wrote:

"When my baby was six months old I placed a border of white cardboard four feet in height around the walls of her nursery. On one side of the wall I placed the letters of the alphabet, which I had cut from red glazed paper. On another wall I formed from the same red letters simple words arranged in rows as bat, cat, hat, mat, rat; bog, dog, hog, log. You will notice that there were only nouns in these lists . . .

"After Winifred had learned all of her letters I began to teach her the words on the wall by spelling them out and making rhymes about them . . .

"Through these games of word building, and the impressions made upon Winifred's mind by reading to her, she learned to read at the age of sixteen months, without having been given a so-called reading lesson. Four of my friends have tried this method and have met with success, as the children who were taught in this way all could read simple English text before they were three years old."

The story of this child and her friends learning to read is by no means unique.

In 1918 another remarkably similar example was reported. This was the case of a child named Martha (sometimes called Millie) whose father, an attorney, began to teach her to read when she was nineteen months old.

Martha lived near Lewis M. Terman, a famous educator. Terman was astonished by the success Martha's father achieved in teaching Martha and he urged her father to write a detailed account of what he had done. This account was published, with an introduction by Terman, in the *Journal of Applied Psychology*, Vol. II (1918).

Coincidentally, Martha's father also used large red block letters for his words as has the author, and as had Winifred's mother.

In writing of her in *Genetic Studies of Genius and Mental and Physical Traits of a Thousand Gifted Children (1925)* Terman said:

"This girl probably holds the world's record for early reading. At the age of twenty-six and a half months her reading vocabulary was above seven hundred words, and as early as twenty-one months she read and apprehended simple sentences as connected thoughts rather than as isolated words. By that age she could distinguish and name all the primary colors.

"By the time she was twenty-three months old she began to experience evident pleasure when she read. At twenty-four months she had a reading vocabulary of over two hundred words, which had increased to more than seven hundred words two and a half months later.

"When she was twenty-five months old she read fluently and with expression to one of us from several primers and first readers that she had never seen before. At this age her reading ability was at least equal to that of the average seven year old who had attended school a year."

In Philadelphia, The Institutes for the Achievement of Human Potential has found it possible to teach even brain-injured children to read well. This does not prove that such children are superior to unhurt children; it simply shows that very young children can learn to read.

And we adults really *should* permit them to do so, if for no other reason than the fact that they enjoy it so much.

4

tiny children
are learning
to read

*It sounds silly to say that he can read when
he's only three years old but when we go to
market he reads the names on so many of the
cans and packages.*

—ALMOST ALL
PARENTS WHO HAVE A THREE-YEAR-OLD

In November of 1962, at a meeting of a group
of educators, physicians and others concerned
with the neurological development of children,
a county supervisor of education told the following
story.

He had been an educator for thirty-five years,
and two weeks before the meeting a kindergarten
teacher had reported that when she prepared to
read a book to her five-year-olds, one of the chil-

dren had volunteered to read it. The teacher pointed out that the book was a new one that the five-year-old had never seen, but he insisted that he could read it anyway. The teacher decided that the easiest way to dissuade the child was to let him try. She did—and he did. He read the entire book aloud to his class, accurately and easily.

The supervisor pointed out that for the first thirty-two years of his life as an educator he had occasionally heard stories about five-year-olds who could read books, but that in all of those three decades he had never actually seen one who could. However, he pointed out, in the last three years there had been at least one child in every kindergarten group who could read.

Thirty-two years of no five-year-olds who could read and then at least one in every one of his kindergartens for the last three years! The educator concluded by stating that he had investigated every case to determine who had taught these children to read.

"Do you know who had taught every one of these children to read?" he asked the child developmentalist who was leading the discussion.

"Yes," said the developmentalist, "I think I do know. The answer is that nobody taught them."

The supervisor agreed that this was the case.

In a sense nobody had taught these children to read, just as in a sense it is true that nobody teaches a child to understand spoken language.

In a broader sense, everybody plus the child's environment had taught the child to read, just as everybody plus the child's environment teaches a child to understand spoken language.

Today television is becoming a standard part of the environment of almost all American children. This is the major factor which had been added to the lives of these kindergarten children.

By watching television commercials which show big clear words accompanied by loud clear pronunciations, children are unconsciously beginning to learn to read. By asking a few key questions of adults who are unaware of what is taking place, this ability to read has been expanded. By having children's books read to them by parents who are attempting only to amuse them, these children have attained astonishing reading vocabularies.

In the cases where parents have become aware of what was actually going on, they have delightedly aided the child in his learning. Generally they have done so despite dire but vague predictions by well-meaning friends that something awful but difficult to classify would happen to the child if they helped him to learn to read before he went to school.

Although we had made no public announcement of our work until mid-1963, there were hundreds of professional visitors to The Institutes as well as postgraduate students of The Institutes who, prior to 1963, were aware of our interest in teaching very young children to read.

In addition there were well over four hundred mothers and fathers of brain-injured children who were at various stages of teaching these children to read under our direction. More than one hundred of these brain-injured children ranged in age from one to five, while another hundred were six years of age and over.

It was inevitable that word of what we were doing should begin to leak out. By the beginning of 1963 we had received hundreds of letters. By the middle of 1963, following an article by the author in a national magazine, we had received thousands of letters.

A surprisingly small percentage of these letters were critical in nature and we shall deal later with those and the questions they raised.

Mothers wrote us letters from all over the United States and from many foreign countries. We were delighted and gratified to learn that a great many parents had taught two- and three-year-olds to read. In some cases they had done so fifteen or more years before. Many of the children so taught were now in college or had graduated. These letters constituted a flood of new evidence about the reading ability of young children.

Here are a few abstracts from some of the letters we received.

Dear Sirs:

... I thought you might be interested to hear that I did teach a baby to read seventeen years ago. I had no real system and in fact did not know at the time that this was very unusual. It came about through my enjoying books myself, reading to the child when she was very young and then being ill for several months so that I needed passive things to do with my two-and-a-half-year-old.

We had a game with letters two or three inches high, and cards with simple words on them. She took an intense interest in these letters, and in finding counterparts in our little books. She even learned some of the letters from sky-writing.

When the child was still of pre-kindergarten age she could read enough in the newspaper to find articles about fires, which scared her; and had certainly long passed primers ...

She is now an honor student in a fine university and, further, a success socially and in sports, as well as in other lines of skills and interest. This is what lies ahead for at least one person who could read before she was three ...

Dear Sir:

... I have seen it proved in my own daughter. She is now fifteen years old ... a sophomore in high school, and has been a straight 'A' student since she was in First Grade.

... She has a wonderful personality and is well liked by her teachers and the students ...

My husband is a disabled veteran of World War I ... Neither of us had enough education to hold a worthwhile job. He went to the 5th grade and I to the 8th. We made a living by traveling and selling small articles house to house ... We bought an 18 foot trailer house ... She was raised in that trailer ... When my daughter was ten months old I bought her her first book ... It was really an ABC book with the objects of what each letter stood for, A for apple, etc. In six months she knew every object and could name them. When she was two years old I got her a larger ABC book (and other books too). While we were traveling it was an excellent time for teaching her. While we were stopped in the different towns she needed something to occupy her mind. If I was selling, my husband had to keep her entertained. She always wanted to know what the different signs spelled ... My husband would tell her ... We never did teach her the alphabet. She learned that later on, in school ... She was started in school on her sixth birthday in the First Grade and it was no trouble at all for her to make A's ... Oh yes, we still live in a trailer house, 34 feet long. One end is for her books ... We have a city library here and she has made a big dent in their book supply.

I know this is a long letter and it may sound like bragging but really it isn't meant to be that. I know if young parents would only take the time, there are plenty of children who could do the same things that our daughter has done, if given the chance. You can't just jerk these kids up and plop them into school at the age of 6 and expect them to learn quickly, without a little foundation work from the time they are babies on up.

... If you think this letter would be of any help to young parents you may print it. If not, that is O.K. anyway. The main thing was I wanted you to know that I know, "You *Can* Teach Your Baby to Read!"

Gentlemen:

... I wish to add that it can be done by an uninformed amateur like myself... my older one accidentally learned the alphabet before he was eighteen months old ...

... about the time he was three he would ask what road signs meant ... and he was reading before he was in kindergarten without much help from me except for answering his questions. Although he is now in first grade and learning to write neatly on that level, he is doing all second grade work in reading and arithmetic and is near the top of the class in these ... does the high I.Q. come as the result of reading early, or does reading early come as the result of a high I.Q.?

... I have never had much time to talk with my second one, and as a result he is not nearly as scholarly ... However, I can not help regretting the fact that I gave my second boy less attention in this respect and it may be a drawback all his life.

... I for one also say that they *love* to learn and can learn a great deal more at an early age when it is just "child's play" to them.

Dear Sir:

... finally giving recognition to the fact that children of two, three and four years of age can be taught to read, and moreover, want to learn to read. My own daughter knew her complete alphabet ... and could read several words at the age of two. A few days after her third birthday she suddenly, it seemed, realized that reading several words in succession produced that complete thought known as a sentence. From that time her reading has progressed rapidly and now, at four and a half, she reads at least as well as most children completing their second grade in school.

An M.D. in Norway made these comments:

Dear Sir:

I have taught 2 of my 3 children to read at 4 and 3 years, by a slightly different method. Your arguments sound very convincing to me. From my experience I think your method definitely better than my own, and I will try to use it with my youngest child (7 months) next year.

... In Norway reading is kept from preschoolers as jealously as information about sex in earlier times. In spite of this I found the following results when I examined 200 preschoolers: 10% were reading fairly well and more than a third knew all the letters.

I think developing the brain is the most important and challenging job of our time, and in my opinion you have done a truly pioneering work.

It must be made clear that these mothers had taught their children to read, or had discovered that their children could read, before the publication of this book and should in no way be construed to be endorsements of the methods outlined in this book. They are simply letters from alert mothers who agree that children *can* learn to read, *are* learning to read and *should* learn to read prior to entering school.

At Yale, Dr. O.K. Moore has for many years been doing extensive research in how to teach preschool children to read. Dr. Moore believes that it is easier to teach a three-year-old to read than a four-year-old, a four-year-old than a five-year-old, a five-year-old than a six-year-old.

Of course it's easier.

It should be.

Yet, how many times have we heard it said that children cannot learn to read until they are six—and that they should not?

About half a century ago a woman named Maria Montessori was the first female to graduate from an Italian medical school. Dr. Montessori became interested in the highly neglected group of children who were loosely classified as "retarded." Such a classification is most unscientific, since there are hundreds of different reasons why a child's development may be held back. Nonetheless, Maria Montessori brought to this pathetically misunderstood group of children both a medical background and a womanly sympathy and appreciation.

Working with such children, she began to appreciate that they could be trained to perform at much higher levels than was at that time the case, and that this was particularly true if such training began earlier than at school age.

Dr. Montessori decided, over a period of years, that these children should be approached through all of the senses and began to teach them through visual, auditory and tactile means. Her results were so gratifying that some of her "retarded" children began to do as well as some normal children. As a result Dr. Montessori concluded that well children were not performing anywhere near their potential and that they should be given an opportunity to do so.

Montessori schools have existed for many years in Europe for subnormal children as well as for normal children. Now there are Montessori schools in the United States, dedicated to helping well children of preschool age achieve their potential. Children are engaged in a broad program at three years of age, and usually the result is that the majority of them are reading words at four.

The oldest Montessori school in the United States is the Whitby School at Greenwich, Connecticut, and a visit to that school reveals a group of delightful, happy, well-adjusted children, learning to read and to perform other tasks which up to now have been considered advanced for preschool children.

One year after the reading program had been introduced at The Institutes, there were 231 brain-injured children learning to read. Of these children, 143 were below six years of age. The rest were six years or older, and could not read prior to the beginning of the program.

These children, who had physical problems as well as language problems, visited The Institutes every sixty days. On the occasion of each visit their neurological development was tested (including their reading ability). The parents were then taught the next step, as described later in this book, and were sent home to continue the physical program as well as the reading schedule.

By the time these *brain-injured* children had been on the program for periods ranging from one visit (60 days) to five visits (10 months) *every child* could read something, ranging from letters of the alphabet to entire books. Many brain-injured three-year-olds in this group could read sentences and books with total understanding.

As has been said, the foregoing does not prove

that brain-injured children are superior to well children, but simply that well children are not achieving what they can and should.

The figures cited do not include the hundreds of reading problems encountered at The Institutes by children who are not brain-injured but who are failing in school because they cannot read. Nor do they include the groups of well two- and three-year-old children whom their parents are teaching to read under the guidance of The Institutes.

At Yale University, as we have seen, Dr. Moore is teaching small children to read.

So do the Montessori schools.

So do The Institutes in Philadelphia.

It is quite possible that other groups, of whom the author is unaware, are also purposely teaching tiny children to read, using an organized system. One result of this book should be to discover what other groups are doing in this very important work.

In virtually all parts of the United States tiny children are learning to read even without their parents' guidance. As a result, we are going to have to make some decisions.

The first decision will have to be whether or not we *want* two- and three-year-old children to read.

If we decide we *don't* want them to be able to read, there are at least two things we have to do:

1. Get rid of television sets, or at least forbid words to be shown on TV.
2. Be careful never to read newspaper headlines or product names to kids.

Now, on the other hand, if we don't want to go to all that trouble, we could take the easy way out and just go right ahead and let them read.

If we do decide to take the easy way out and to permit three-year-olds to read, we certainly should do something about *what* they read.

We believe that the best way is to teach them to read at home with the parents' help rather than through television. It is easy, and the parents enjoy it almost as much as the children.

Whether children are learning to read or not isn't a theory which we may argue. It is a fact. The only question is what we are going to do about it.

5

tiny children should learn to read

Do you not know, then, that the beginning in every task is the chief thing, especially for any creature that is young and tender? For it is then that it is best molded and takes the impression that one wishes to stamp upon it.

—PLATO

Herbert Spencer said that the brain should not be starved any more than the stomach. Education should begin in the cradle, but in an interesting atmosphere. The man to whom information comes in dreary tasks along with threats of punishment is unlikely to be a student in after years, while those to whom it comes in natural forms, at the proper times, are likely to continue through life that self-instruction begun in youth.

We have already discussed several children who were successfully taught by their mothers and who later developed splendidly, but those are not examples from the professional literature.

Let's now examine the results of the case of Millie (Martha), reported by Terman later in the life of this child.

By the time Millie was twelve years and eight months old she was two years ahead of children her own age, being in the last half of the ninth grade. Terman reports:

"In the previous semester she was the only pupil in lower nine class of about 40 to make the high school honor roll.

"In our 1927–28 follow-up, the first thing the field visitor asked Millie's teacher was what subject she excelled in. The answer was, 'Millie reads beautifully.' In a chat with the field visitor Millie said she 'would like to read five books a day if it weren't for going to school.' She also admitted simply and without self-consciousness that she could read very fast, had read through Markham's thirteen volumes of the *Real American Romance* in a week. Her father, doubting whether she could read these books so rapidly and still assimilate them, asked her questions about the material read. She was able to answer them to his satisfaction."

Terman concludes that there is no evidence to indicate that Millie was in any way harmed by her being taught to read as a baby, and much evidence to support the view that her high abilities were due at least in part to her early training.

Her various I.Q. test scores averaged to above 140, and she was strong and lively. She suffered no handicaps in social adaptability even though her classmates were two or three years her senior.

An I.Q. of 140 placed Millie in the genius category.

Many studies indicate that a very high number of superior adults and geniuses were able to read long before they went to school. It has always been assumed that these people could read at such a young age *because* they were superior people. This is a perfectly proper scientific premise and we have always accepted it.

However, in light of the many instances on record where parents have decided to teach tiny children to read long before it was possible to make a valid test of their intelligence, and therefore before there was any reason to assume that a child would be superior, we must now raise some new questions.

Is it not that these children became superior *because* they were taught to read at an early age?

The fact that there are so many superior persons, and indeed geniuses, who could read before they were of school age, supports either the first or second assumption equally well.

There is, however, more evidence to support the second premise than there is to support the first, and it too is a perfectly valid scientific supposition.

The assumption that many highly intelligent people could read at a very young age *because* they are geniuses rests essentially on a genetic basis and presumes that all such people are superior because they were genetically endowed with this potential.

We would not dispute the fact that there are genetic differences in people, nor would we care to become deeply involved with the age-old discussion of how much environment weighs when measured against genetics, since it does not directly concern the primary point of this book.

Still, we cannot close our eyes to the considerable evidence which supports the possibility that early reading has a strong influence on performance in later life.

a. Many children who turned out to be superior were taught to read before there was any evidence that they were in any way unusual. Indeed, some parents had decided before a child was born that they would make the child superior by teaching it to read at an early age, and did so.

b. In many of the recorded cases one child was

taught to read and later proved to be superior, while other children in the *same* family with the *same* parents were not taught to read early and did not become superior. In some cases the child taught to read was the first child. In other families, for various reasons, the child who learned to read early was not the first child.

c. In the case of Tommy Lunski (and there are other cases similar to his) there was certainly nothing to indicate that Tommy would have any special genetic endowment. Tommy's parents both have less than a high school education and are in no way intellectually unusual. Tommy's brothers and sisters are average children. In addition to all this, it should be recalled that Tommy was very severely brain-injured, and at two years of age it was recommended that he be placed in an institution for life as "hopelessly retarded." There is no question but that today Tommy is an extraordinary child who reads and comprehends at least as well as the average child more than twice his age.

Would it be fair, scientific or even rational to refer to Tommy as a "gifted" child?

Thomas Edison said that genius is 10 per cent inspiration and 90 per cent perspiration. (It is interesting to note that the young Thomas Edison himself was considered to be "retarded" as a child.)

We have already discussed in some detail the six neurological functions which belong exclusively to human beings, and have pointed out that three of these are *receptive* abilities while the other three are *expressive*.

It seems obvious that man's intelligence is limited to the information he can gain from the world through his receptive senses. The highest of these receptive abilities is the ability to read.

It is equally obvious that if all three of man's receptive abilities were totally cut off, he would be more of a vegetable than a human being.

Man's intelligence, then, is limited by the sum of the three uniquely human characteristics of seeing and hearing in a manner that culminates in the ability to read and to understand spoken language, and a special ability to feel that enables him, if necessary, to read language by feeling.

Destroy these three receptive abilities and you destroy most of what makes man different from other animals.

Limit these three abilities and you will equally limit a human's intelligence.

Unless one of these three human abilities is high, we will see a human being whose intelligence is low.

If one of these abilities is higher than the others,

the person will perform to the top level of that ability, *provided every conceivable opportunity is made available to that person to gain information through that single facility.*

No person will rise above the highest receptive ability he has plus the opportunity he is given to use that receptive ability.

The reverse is, of course, equally true. If all three of these abilities in a single human being are low, then that human being will perform at a very low, and indeed subhuman, level.

If we could imagine a situation in which man suddenly lost his ability to read and to hear language, it would be necessary to teach the new generation to communicate in some other way. It is obvious that we would choose the sense of touch to communicate, as did Helen Keller's first teacher, since her pupil, because of blindness and deafness, could not speak, read or write. If Helen Keller's ability to receive language through the sense of touch had been very low, she could have existed only at an animal level. Had her sense of touch been nonexistent, as was her sight and hearing, she would have existed at a vegetable level.

When these capacities are increased in man, his ability to perform will be increased.

Certainly the severely brain-injured children who were taught to read at a very early age have demonstrated far greater ability than the brain-injured children who were not given such an opportunity. And the well children whose cases have been cited, and many others, appear to have performed at much higher levels than their peers who were not given such an opportunity.

It may be true that there are some adult idiots who can understand language in a limited way, but there are no geniuses who *cannot* understand language—not in our culture at any rate.

Of course it must be borne in mind that intelligence can only be related to the culture in which it exists. A normal adult Australian aborigine brought to New York City and given an ordinary American intelligence test would be found to be an idiot by our standards.

On the other hand, an adult American taken to a tribe of Australian aborigines would be almost helpless in that culture and would probably not even survive unless cared for by those people, much in the manner we care for our idiots. Obviously the American "idiot" would be unable to get food with a boomerang, unable to catch live lizards and eat them raw, unable to find water, and, particularly, unable to understand what he was being told—at least for a while.

Language is the most important tool available to man. Man can have no more sophisticated thoughts than he has language to formulate them.

If he needs additional words, he must invent them to use as tools for thinking and communicating the new thought.

This is easily seen in our technical society, where thousands of words must be invented each decade to describe man's new devices. During World War II, the Fifth Air Force trained a large group of American Indians in radio techniques and sent them to units in the Pacific. Since few if any Japanese could speak Choctaw or Sioux, it was hoped that valuable time could be saved by not having to code messages.

It did not work. There were simply no words in the Indian languages to describe a fighter bomber, a torpedo plane, an aircraft carrier, fuel injection, or countless other Air Force terms.

Virtually all tests of intelligence applied to human beings are dependent upon the ability to take in written information (reading) or upon the ability to take in spoken information. In our culture this is as it should be.

If the ability to read is reduced or nonexistent, there is no question but that the ability to express intelligence is also markedly diminished.

Among the peoples of the earth who do not have a written language, or where the written language is crude, it is not only true that such tribes are uneducated but it is also true that their intelligence and creativity are low.

Eskimo babies are sewn into the furs on Mother's back and are denied virtually all opportunity to crawl or creep until they are close to three years of age. This becomes highly interesting when we appreciate that the Eskimo culture has remained virtually unchanged for at least the three thousand years that it can be traced back. The Eskimo has *no* written language. The spoken Eskimo tongue is a very crude one.

While it is obvious that lack of material to read, or the lack of ability to read it, inevitably results in lack of education, it is infinitely more important that it also results in lower intelligence.

It is a purely academic question to inquire whether the Australian aborigines don't read because they are of low intelligence or whether they are of low intelligence because they do not read.

Lack of reading and lack of intelligence go hand in hand both in individuals and in nations.

The converse is also true.

Language ability is a vital tool. One cannot imagine conducting a sophisticated conversation or describing a complicated thought in the language of an Amazonian tribe, even if one spoke the language fluently.

The ability to express intelligence is therefore related to the facility of the language with which one is dealing.

There is no truly valid test of I.Q. in children below the age of two and a half years. One can start applying the Stanford-Binet test to a child two and a half years old and achieve results which may prove generally valid later in life. As language ability increases, however, the tests which are applied become more valid, and later such tests as the Wechsler-Bellevue may be used.

Naturally, the language proficiency required of a child in I.Q. testing is higher each year. It is therefore clear that if a child's verbal competence is more advanced than that of other children of the same age, he will test, and be considered, more intelligent than the other children.

Tommy Lunski was classified as a hopeless idiot at two, *essentially because he could not talk* (and thus express his intelligence), while he was considered to be a superior child at five *because he could read superbly.*

It is completely clear that the ability to read, and at an early age, has much to do with the measurement of intelligence. In the end it matters little whether the ability to express intelligence is a valid test of intelligence itself—it is the test upon which intelligence is judged.

The earlier a child reads, the more he is likely to read and the better he reads.

Some of the reasons, then, that children should learn to read when they are very young are as follows:

a. The hyperactivity of the two- and three-year-old child is, in fact, the result of a boundless thirst for knowledge. If he is given an opportunity to quench that thirst, at least for a small part of the time, he will be far less hyperactive, far easier to protect from harm, and far better able to learn about the world when he is moving about and learning about the physical world and himself.

b. The child's ability to take in information at two and three years of age will never be equaled again.

c. It is infinitely easier to teach a child to read at this age than it will ever be again.

d. Children taught to read at a very young age absorb a great deal *more information* than do children whose early attempts to learn are frustrated.

e. Children who learn to read while very young tend to comprehend better than youngsters who do not. It is interesting to listen to the three-year-old, who reads with inflection and meaning, in contrast to the average seven-year-old, who reads each word separately and without appreciation of the sentence as a whole.

f. Children who learn to read while very young tend to read much more rapidly and comprehensively than children who do not. This is because young children are much less awed by reading and do not consider it a "subject" full of frightening abstractions. Tiny children view it as just another fascinating thing in a world jammed with fascinating things to be learned. They do not "hang up" on the details but deal with reading in a totally functional sense. They are very right to do so.

g. Finally, and at least as important as the above stated reasons—children love to learn to read at a very early age.

6

who has problems,
readers or
nonreaders?

*Many of these children are ordinarily classi-
fied as gifted, but where records are adequate
all precocious readers received a great deal of
prior stimulation. Consequently, to label a
child as gifted in no way dispenses with the
necessity of stimulation . . . if he is to learn.*

—WILLIAM FOWLER, *Cognitive
Learning in Infancy and Early Childhood*

There was a strong temptation to entitle this chapter "Something Awful Is Going to Happen," since
its purpose is to cover the dire predictions concern-
ing what will happen to youngsters who read too
soon. It was also tempting to call this chapter
"Nobody Listens to Mothers," which is at least
part of the reason why so many myths arise about
youngsters.

There is a myth abroad in the land which holds

that only experts of one kind or another understand children. Among the innumerable kinds of
experts who deal with children there are too many
who insist that mothers

a. don't know much about children;
b. are completely inaccurate observers of their
   own children;
c. tell awful lies about their own children's
   abilities.

In our own experience nothing could be further
from the truth.

While we have met some mothers who tell fantastic and untrue stories about their children and
who do not understand them, we think they are
very rare indeed. Rather, we have found mothers
to be careful and sound observers of their own
children, and they are, besides, absolutely stark
realists.

The trouble is that hardly anybody listens to
mothers.

At The Institutes we see more than a thousand
brain-injured children each year. There is hardly
anything a mother fears more than having a brain-
injured child. And if she suspects it, she wants to
find out at the first possible moment so she can
start doing immediately whatever has to be done.

In over nine hundred out of a thousand cases

seen at The Institutes, it was Mother who first decided that *something* was wrong with her baby. In most cases Mother had a very difficult time convincing anyone—including the family doctor and other professional people—that something was wrong and that something should be done about it at that instant.

No matter how hard or how long everyone tries to talk her out of it she persists until the situation is recognized. Sometimes it takes her years. The more she loves her baby, the more detached she makes herself in evaluating its condition. If the child has a problem, she will not rest until it is solved.

At The Institutes we have learned to listen to mothers.

However, when dealing with well children, many professionals have succeeded in thoroughly intimidating mothers. They have frequently managed to get mothers to parrot a great deal of professional jargon which is often not even understood. Worst of all, they have come close to blunting mothers' instinctive reactions to their growing children, convincing them that they are being betrayed by their maternal instincts.

If this trend continues, we run the serious risk of persuading mothers to view their offspring not as children at all but instead as little bundles of strange ego drives and dark, rather nasty packages

of strange and frightening symbolisms that an un-
trained mother couldn't possibly understand.

Nonsense. In our experience mothers make the
very best mothers there are.

Nowhere have we jammed more myths and
fears down mothers' throats, or forced mothers to
thwart all their maternal instincts, than in the area
of preschool learning.

Today many mothers have come to believe
things which they think are true simply because
they have been repeated so often. We shall try to
deal seriously with these common statements, all
of which are myths to one degree or another.

1. *The Myth:* Children who read too early will
   have learning problems.
   The Fact: In none of the children we know
   personally, nor in any of the children we
   have read about who were taught at home,
   have we found this to be the case. In fact, in
   the vast majority of the cases precisely the
   reverse is true. Many of the results of early
   reading have already been described.

   It is difficult to understand why there is
   so much surprise over the fact that such a
   high percentage of children have a reading
   problem. It is not at all surprising. What is
   surprising is that *anyone* learns to read, start-

ing as most do when the capacity to learn easily and naturally is just about over.

2. *The Myth:* Children who read too early will be nasty little geniuses.

   The Fact: Come, come, myth makers, let's get together. Are the early readers going to be dunces or geniuses? It's surprising, really, how often the same person will tell Myth #1 and also Myth #2. The fact is that neither is true. Where we have seen early readers we have seen happy, well-adjusted children who had more to enjoy than other children. We do not hold that early reading will *solve* all of the problems which might beset a child, and we suppose if you looked far enough you might find a child who was an early reader and who for other reasons also happened to be a nasty kid. In our experience you would have to look further for such a child among the early readers than you would among those who learned to read in school. We are quite confident that you could find many, many unhappy and badly adjusted children among those who *cannot* read when they start school. They are very common indeed.

3. *The Myth:* The child who reads too early will cause problems in first grade.

   The Fact: This is not wholly a myth, for it is partly true. He will cause problems at first.

Not for *him,* but for the teacher. Since schools are meant to be for the good of the child rather than for the teacher, it will be necessary for the teacher to exercise a bit of effort to solve her problem. Daily, hundreds of fine teachers are doing just that, with ease. It is the few teachers not willing to make a small degree of effort who are largely responsible for keeping this complaint in circulation. But any teacher worth her salt can handle the advanced reader with a fraction of the time and effort necessary to cope with the problems of the legion of kids who *can't* read. As a matter of fact, a first-grade teacher with a class full of children who can read and who love it would have relatively few problems. This situation would also solve many problems later on, since much time is spent in *all* grades dealing with nonreaders.

It's too bad that the first-grade teacher can't solve all of her problems (and she has dozens of them) as easily as she can cope with the child who can read when he arrives in first grade. Hundreds of good first-grade teachers solve this problem very simply by giving the child books to read by himself while she struggles through the alphabet with his classmates. Many teachers go further and actually have the child read aloud to his classmates. He generally enjoys the opportunity to demonstrate his ability, and the other children are less awed when they see that it can be done. Good teachers have many approaches to this "problem."

What do we do about unimaginative teachers? That is a problem, isn't it? It's a problem for *all* the children in any class that has a poor teacher. The chances are excellent that the following will happen when a first-grade class has such a teacher: The child who will be the best in second grade is the one who could read before he started school. He didn't need first grade nearly as much as the other children.

Ironically, even the school that objects the most to a child who can read before he enters first grade is extremely proud of a child who is a superior reader in the *second* grade. One of the easiest problems that any sensible first-grade teacher has to deal with is what to do with the child who *can* read. The most difficult problem for her, and the most time-consuming, is the child she *can't* teach to read.

Even if all this were not true, would anyone seriously argue that we should prevent a child from learning in order to keep him at the average level of his classmates?

4. *The Myth:* The child who learns to read too early will be bored in first grade.

The Fact: This is the fear that concerns the

vast majority of mothers and is the question that is most sensible of all. To state it more accurately, what we are really asking here is, "Won't the child who has learned *too much* be bored in first grade?"

The answer to this is that, yes, there is a good chance he'll be bored silly in first grade *just like almost every other kid in first grade.* Did the reader ever live through days half as long as those he spent in first grade? Schools by and large are much better today than they were when the reader of this book went to school. But ask almost any first grader how long a school day is as compared to Saturday or Sunday. Does his answer mean that he doesn't want to learn? Not at all, but when five-year-olds carry on the sophisticated conversations that they do, can we really expect them to get very pepped up when they read such enduring material as "See the automobile. It is a pretty red automobile." The seven-year-old who has to read such sentences can not only see the pretty red automobile, he can tell you the manufacturer, the year, the body type and probably the horsepower. If there is anything else you'd like to know about the pretty red automobile, just ask him. He knows more about it than you do. Children will go right on being bored in school until we give them material worthy of their interest.

To assume that the child who knows the most will be the most bored is to assume that the child who knows the least is the most interested and therefore the least bored. If the class is uninteresting, all will be bored. If it is interesting, only the ones who are not able to understand will be bored.

5. *The Myth:* The child who learns to read too early will miss phonetics.

The Fact: He may miss phonetics, but if he does he won't miss it. The foregoing may be a bad play on words, but it is a fact.

Dr. O.K. Moore, who has been mentioned previously as one of the true pioneers in teaching three-year-olds to read, has refused to be drawn into the perpetual and extremely peripheral battle which rages in the controversy between the advocates of the "look-say" approach to reading and the "phonics" approach to reading. He has termed this a sterile fight.

At the present time there is no "best" way to teach very young children to read. There is certainly no exclusive method, any more than there is one to teach a child to learn language through his ear. You might well ask yourself, "Did I teach my child to hear by the 'phonics' method or the 'listen-hear' method, or did I simply expose him to spoken language?" You might ask also, "How well did he do?" If he learned to hear and speak language fairly well, maybe the system you used was a pretty good system.

The materials which we at The Institutes use to help tiny children to learn to read contain no black magic, or red magic either. They are simply a neat, orderly, organized approach to teaching a child how to read. They are based on an understanding of how a child's brain grows and on experience with a great many normal as well as hurt children. They are simply *a* way which has the virtue of working with a very high percentage of tiny children.

Yes, it's true. Your child may miss phonics if you teach him to read when he's tiny—and won't that be nice.

6. *The Myth:* The child who reads too early will have a reading problem.

The Fact: He may, but his chances will be far smaller of having a reading problem than they will be if he learns to read at the usual time.

Children who *can* read don't have reading problems. Those who *can't* read have the problems.

7. *The Myth:* The child who reads too early will
be deprived of his precious childhood.
The Fact: Of all the taboos which have been
built up around children and reading this is
the most patent piece of nonsense. Let's look
at life for a minute and examine the facts,
not a group of illusory fairy tales.

Is the average two- or three-year-old child
occupied every minute of the day, having the
most delightful time doing what he enjoys
more than anything else? What he likes the
most is spending every possible minute at
work and play with his family. Nothing, just
nothing, can compare with his family's
undivided attention, and if he had his way
that's the way he'd arrange it.

But what child in our society, our culture
and our time ever has such a childhood?
Little practical details keep interfering. Details like: Who is going to clean the house,
who is going to do the laundry, who is going
to do the ironing, who is going to cook the
dinner, who is going to do the dishes, who is
going to do the shopping? In most homes that
we know of, it is Mom who does these things.

Sometimes, if Mom is clever enough, and
if Mom is patient enough, she can find ways
to do some of these things with her two-year-
old, like introducing him to the wonderful

game of doing the dishes. When she can, it is an elegant thing to do.

However, the vast majority of the mothers we know have not been able to share all their chores with their children. The result of all this is that the average two-year-old spends a high percentage of his time screaming in anguish to get out of the play pen. Mother simply had to put him there so that he wouldn't electrocute himself, get crushed, cut himself, or fall out the window while she got something done.

Is this the precious childhood we're talking about wasting while he learns to read? It is, more or less, in practically every home we know. If it isn't the case in *your* home, and you are one of the people who can and does give your attention almost every moment of the day to your two-year-old, then we think you have nothing to worry about and that there is a good chance your two-year-old already knows how to read. You can't spend all day, every day, teaching him to patty cake.

We haven't met a single mother, no matter how busy, who doesn't make it a point to find some time to spend with her child during every day of the child's early years. The question is how to spend that time most fruitfully, most happily and most usefully. Certainly it's true that we don't want to waste a minute that will help to create a happier, more capable, more creative child.

We who have spent our lives as staff members of an organization which deals with the development of children are persuaded that there is no more productive and joyful way for mother and tiny child to occupy a few minutes together each day than in the pursuit of reading.

The joy that parent and child know as the child learns what words, sentences and books mean has no parallel. This is one of the great fulfillments of a truly precious childhood.

Let us conclude by returning to Millie and her parents. In his published account of Millie, her father stated part of the case correctly and succinctly when he said, "If learning to read had not occupied the baby's mind, some other less fruitful activity would have."

But Millie's mother, exercising her female prerogative, had the last and perhaps most important word: "We enjoy each other so much that we don't seem to care about having others along, but I'm afraid it's rather selfish of us."

8. *The Myth:* The child who reads too early will suffer from "too much pressure."

The Fact: If this myth means that it is possible to bring too much pressure on a child by teaching him to read, then it is certainly true. It is equally true that we can put too much pressure on a child by teaching him anything else.

Pressuring a child for any reason is a foolish thing to do and we urgently advise all parents against it. So don't. Now the question here is, what does pressuring have to do with providing a child with an opportunity to learn to read? If the reader decides that he or she would like to follow the advice contained in this book, the answer is that there is no connection between pressure and how a child should learn to read. Indeed, we not only advise parents *not* to pressure their children but insist that unless *both* parent and child are in the right frame of mind and eager to read, the child should not even be *permitted* to read.

There are probably a great number of additional ghost stories about the awful things that will happen if you teach a tiny child to read, but in all of our experience we have never seen one single unhappy result. All of the dire predictions we have heard are based on the lack of understanding of the process of brain development, of which reading should be a part.

In line with this, we might reiterate one of the most important points that this book seeks to make. Simply stated, and from a neurological standpoint, reading is not a school subject at all: It is a brain function.

Reading language is a brain function exactly as hearing language is a brain function.

What would our reaction be if, in examining a child's classroom subjects, we found geography, spelling, civics and hearing?

Surely we would say, what is hearing doing there, listed as a school subject? Hearing, we would surely say, is something the brain does, not to be confused with subjects taught in school.

So is reading.

Spelling, on the other hand, *is* a proper school subject.

A child may be a splendid reader and not necessarily a good speller. They are two different things and two totally diverse processes. Reading is something the brain does, and spelling is a subject about certain rules people have invented to help keep reading and writing orderly. When the teacher teaches spelling, she is passing on facts from the body of knowledge which man has accumulated. When a child reads, his brain is not dealing with the details of how a word is constructed. The child's brain is actually interpreting thoughts, expressed by the writer.

Let the reader ask himself two questions:

1. Can he read any words he is unable to spell? Of course he can—many.
2. Can he spell any words he cannot read? Of course he cannot. Reading is a brain function, and spelling is a set of rules. Just as we can read and understand words that we can't spell, we can even read and understand words that we cannot pronounce. The authors recently heard a learned professor with a Ph.D. mispronounce the word "epitome." He had obviously been using the word for years and using it correctly. Even if he had been trained phonetically (and he probably had been), he would still have mispronounced this word. He had simply learned it by reading, as we learn the vast majority of the roughly one hundred thousand words that comprise a decent vocabulary. How many of those words were we actually *taught* in school? Only a small percentage. We come to school with a tremendous speaking vocabulary. We are taught to read, at the most, a few thousand words, and to spell, at the most, a few thousand more. The remaining tens of thousands we have come to know, we have taught ourselves by listening, by reading and, very occasionally, by looking some up in the dictionary.

By all of the above, do we mean to imply that we are opposed to children learning how to spell? Of course not. Spelling is a very proper subject for school and a most important one.

Perhaps, one day in the future, everyone will come to the conclusion that young children should learn to read at home just as they presently learn to hear at home. What a blessing that would be for the privileged mother, for the fortunate child, for the terribly overworked teacher (who could then spend her time transmitting to her pupils the superb store of knowledge man has accumulated). And what a blessing it would also be for our under-financed, underhoused, understaffed school systems.

Look around and see who are the *real* problems in school.

Look at the ten top children in each class in school and see what common factor is the most prominent in the group. That's easy—they are the best readers.

The *nonreading* children are the greatest problem in American education.

7

how to teach
your baby
to read

*We mothers are the potters and our children
the clay.*

—WINIFRED SACKVILLE STONER,
Natural Education

Most sets of instructions begin by saying that unless
they are followed precisely, they won't work.

In contrast to that, it is almost safe to say that no
matter how poorly you expose your baby to reading, he is almost sure to learn more than he would
if you hadn't done it; so this is one game which you
will win to some degree no matter how badly you

play it. You would have to do it incredibly badly to produce no result.

Nonetheless, the more cleverly you play the game of teaching your tiny child to read, the more quickly and the better he will learn to read.

If you play correctly the game of learning to read, both you and your child will enjoy it immensely.

It takes less than a half-hour a day.

Let's review the cardinal points to remember about the child himself before discussing how to teach him to read.

1. The child below the age of five can easily absorb tremendous amounts of information. If the child is below four it will be easier and more effective, below three even easier and much more effective and below two is the easier and the most effective of all.
2. The child below five can accept information at a remarkable rate.
3. The more information a child absorbs below the age of five, the more he retains.
4. The child below five has a tremendous amount of energy.
5. The child below five has a monumental desire to learn.

6. The child below five can learn to read and wants to learn to read.

7. The child below five learns an entire language and can learn almost as many as are presented to him. He can learn to read one language or several just as readily as he understands the spoken language.

AT WHAT AGE TO BEGIN

The question as to when to begin to teach a child to read is a fascinating one. When is a child ready to learn anything?

Once a mother asked a famous child developmentalist at what age she should begin to train her child.

"When," he asked, "will your child be born?"

"Oh, he is five years old now," said the mother.

"Madam, run home quickly. You have wasted the best five years of his life," said the expert.

Beyond two years of age, reading gets harder every year. If your child is five, it will be easier than it would be if he were six. Four is easier still, and three is even easier.

One year of age is the best time to begin if you want to expend the least amount of time and energy in teaching your child to read. (Should you be willing to go to a little trouble you can begin at *eight months* or if you are very clever at *three months* of age.)

There are two *vital* points involved in teaching your child:

a. Your attitude and approach.

b. The size and orderliness of the reading matter.

1. Parent Attitude and Approach

Learning is the greatest adventure in life. Learning is desirable, vital, unavoidable and, above all, life's greatest and most stimulating game. The child believes this and will always believe this—unless we persuade him that it isn't true.

The cardinal rule is that both parent and child must joyously approach learning to read, as the superb game that it is. The parent must never forget that learning is life's most exciting game—it is not work. Learning is a reward, it is not a punishment. Learning is a pleasure, it is not a chore. Learning is a privilege, it is not a denial.

The parent must always remember this, and he must never do anything to destroy this natural attitude in the child.

Only well behaved children should be given the opportunity to play the reading game; badly behaved children should be denied the opportunity. Therefore, if the child has behaved badly, it will not do for the parent to tell the child he has been a good boy and may therefore play the game, just because the parent wants to play it himself. The child won't be fooled for an instant. He knows that he has behaved badly and he may come to the conclusion that reading must be a punishment rather than a reward. If the child has been behaving badly three days in a row he simply doesn't get to play the game for that period of time, no matter how much the parent may look forward to it.

The second important thing is to make sure that the length of time you play the game is very short. At first it will be played 3 times a day, but each session will involve just a few seconds only.

In regard to determining when to end each session of learning, the parent should exercise great ingenuity.

The parent must know what the child is thinking a little bit before the child knows it, and must stop each session well *before* the child wants to stop.

If the parent always observes this fact, the child will beg the parent to play the reading game and the parent will be nurturing rather than destroying the child's natural desire to learn.

In summary, the parent should consistently remember two things:

1. Learning is more fun than anything else.
2. Sessions should always end *before* your child wants to stop.

2. Suitable Materials

The materials used in teaching your child to read are extremely simple. They are based on many years of work on the part of a very large team of human developmentalists and other scientists who were studying how the human brain grows and functions. They are designed in complete recognition of the fact that reading is a brain function. They recognize the capabilities and limitations of the tiny child's visual apparatus and are designed to meet all of his needs from visual crudeness to visual sophistication and from brain function to brain learning.

All materials should be made on fairly stiff white cardboard so that they will stand up under the not-always-gentle handling they will receive.

Such stiff cardboard can be obtained in stationery stores and is referred to as "posterboard." It can be bought in large sheets and cut to shape.

The words used should be lettered with felt tipped markers which are presently on the market under various trade names.

The printing should be neat and clear and have consistent, plain lettering style.

A margin of at least ½″ should be maintained all around the various cards.

The materials used should contain the following components:

1. The words *mommy, daddy* and your child's name on separate cards in addition to twelve other words (described under the First Step on page 111), 6″ high by 24″ long. The letters should be 5″ by 4″ with approximately ½″ between letters; they should be red and printed in lower-case.

mommy

2. The twenty basic "self" words (listed under the Second Step, p. 119) on white cards 5″

high, approximately 24″ long, in red lower-case letters 4″ high.

hand

3. The basic words of the child's immediate world (listed under the Third Step, pp 125) on white cards 3″ high, in red lower-case letters 2″ high.

chair

4. The sentence-structure vocabulary: single-word cards 3″ high, with black lower-case words 2″ high (p. 131).

who

5. The structured-phrase vocabulary: phrase cards with words printed in black lower-case letters 1″ high. These cards are punched and assembled into a book by the use of 1″ loose-leaf rings. The cards must therefore be large enough to accommodate the text of each page (p. 137).

Here is

Tommy

6. A book using a limited vocabulary printed in black upper and lower-case letters ¼ ″ high (p. 139).

The materials begin with large red lower-case letters and progressively change to normal-size black lower-case letters. This is done so that the child's visual pathway may mature and gradually appreciate the material which is being presented to his brain.

The large letters are used initially for the very simple reason that they are most easily seen. They are red simply because red attracts a small child.

You may find it simpler, and in the long run cheaper, to buy a ready-made kit. The Teach Your Baby To Read Kits may be obtained by writing to The Better Baby Press at 8801 Stenton Avenue, Philadelphia, Pa. 19118.

THE FIRST STEP (Visual Differentiation)

The first step in teaching your child to read begins with the use of just fifteen words. When your child has learned these fifteen words he is ready to progress to the vocabularies themselves.

Begin at a time of day when the child is receptive, rested and in a good mood.

Use a part of the house that has as few distracting factors as possible, in both an auditory and visual sense; for instance, do *not* have the radio playing, and avoid other sources of noise. Use a corner of a room which does not have a great deal of furniture, pictures or other objects which might distract the child's vision.

Now simply hold up the word *mommy,* just beyond his reach, and say to him clearly, "This says 'Mommy.' "

Give the child no more description and do not elaborate. Permit him to see it for no more than one second.

Next, hold up the word *daddy* and say, "This says 'Daddy'."

Show three other words in precisely the same way as you have the first two. Do not ask your child to repeat the words as you go along. After the fifth word, give your child a huge hug and kiss and display your affection in the most obvious ways.

Repeat this three times during the first day, in exactly the manner described above. Sessions should be at least one half-hour apart.

The first day is now over and you have taken the first step in teaching your child to read. (You have thus far invested at most three minutes.)

The second day, repeat the basic session three times. Add a second set of five new words. This new set should be seen three times throughout the day, just like the first set, making a total of six sessions.

At the end of each session tell your child he is very good and very bright. Tell your child that you are very proud of him. Tell him that you love him very much. It is wise to hug him and to express your love for him physically.

Children learn at lightning speed and if you show him the words more than three times a day you will bore him. If you show him a single card for more than a second you will lose him.

Do *not* test him. Not yet. Babies love to learn but they hate to be tested and in that way they are very like grownups. Testing is the opposite of learning. It is full of stress. To teach a child is to give him a delightful gift, to test him is to demand payment— in advance. The more you test him the slower he will learn and the less he'll want to. The less you test him the quicker he will learn and the more he will want to learn. Knowledge is the most precious gift you can give your child. Give it as generously as you give him food. If you must test your child before he voluntarily demonstrates to you that he has learned faster than you believed possible, don't do it quite yet.

Do *not* bribe him or reward him with cookies, candy or the like. At the rate he will be learning in a very short time, you will not be able to afford enough cookies from a financial standpoint, and he

will not be able to take them from a health standpoint. Besides, cookies are a meager reward for
such a major accomplishment, compared with love
and respect.

On the third day, add a third set of five new
words.

Now you are teaching your child three sets of
reading words, five words in each set, each set three
times a day. You and your child are now enjoying
a total of nine reading sessions spread out during
the day, equaling a few minutes in all.

If you have been able to resist testing he may by
now have demonstrated his ability to read words
spontaneously. In either case trust him a bit longer.

Repeat this exact process on days four, five and
six.

On the seventh day, you may wish to give your
child the opportunity to show you how well he is
doing. Pick one of his favorite words. Hold the word
up to the child and say very clearly, "What is this?"

You count to ten slowly and silently.

If your child says the word, you must then be
delighted and make a great fuss. Tell your child he
is very good and very bright. Tell him that you are
very proud of him. Tell him that you love him very
much. It is wise to hug him and to express your love
for him physically. If perchance, he does not re-

spond or does so incorrectly, simply tell him enthusiastically what the word is—and go on.

This opportunity session is an elegant way for your child to demonstrate his success in reading and for you to share in his great accomplishment. If both you and your child thoroughly enjoy this opportunity then it can be used but should never be abused. Don't be tempted to overdo it no matter how much fun it is.

If for any reason you or your child do not enjoy doing this, don't do it.

These opportunities for feedback are actually for you. Your child will be most interested in learning new words and not in going back over old ones he already knows.

The first fifteen words that you teach your child should be made up of the most familiar and enjoyable words around him. These words should include the names of immediate family members, relatives, family pets, favorite foods, objects in the house, and favorite activities. It is impossible to include an exact list here since each child's first fifteen words will be personal and therefore different.

The only warning sign in the entire process of learning to read is boredom. *Never bore the child. Going too slowly is much more likely to bore him than going too quickly.* Remember that this bright baby can be learning, say, Portuguese at this time, so don't bore him. Consider the splendid thing you have just accomplished. Your child has just conquered the most difficult thing he will have to do in the entire business of reading.

He has done, with your help, two most extraordinary things:

1. He has trained his visual pathway and, more importantly, his brain, sufficiently to differentiate between one written symbol and another.
2. He has mastered one of the most staggering abstractions he will ever have to deal with in life: he can read words. He will have to master only one greater abstraction and that is the individual letters of the alphabet.

A word about the alphabet. Why have we not begun by teaching this child the alphabet? The answer to this question is most important.

It is a basic tenet of all teaching that it should begin with the known and the concrete, and progress from this to the new and the unknown, and last of all, to what is abstract.

Nothing could be more abstract to the two-year-old brain than the letter *a*. It is a tribute to the genius of children that they ever learn it.

It is obvious that if the two-year-old were only

more capable of reasoned argument he would long since have made this situation clear to the adults.

If such were the case, when we presented him with the letter *a*, he would ask, "Why is that thing 'a'?"

What would we answer?

"Well," we would say, "it is 'a' because . . . uh . . . because, don't you see it's 'a' because . . . well, because it was necessary to invent this . . . ah . . . symbol to . . . ah . . . stand for the sound 'a' which . . . ah . . . we also invented so that . . . ah . . ."

And so it would have gone.

In the end most of us would surely say, "It is 'a' because I'm bigger than you, that's why it's 'a'!"

And perhaps that's as good a reason as any as to why "a" is "a."

Happily, we haven't had to explain it to the kids because, while perhaps they could not understand historically why "a" is "a," they do know that we are bigger than they, and this reason they would feel to be sufficient.

At any rate, they have managed to learn these twenty-six visual abstractions and, what is more, twenty-six auditory abstractions to go with them. This does not add up to fifty-two possible combinations of sound and picture but instead to 676 possible combinations of abstractions.

All this they learn even though we usually teach

them at five or six, when it's getting a lot harder for them to learn.

Thank goodness we are wise enough not to try to start law students, medical students, or engineering students with any such wild abstractions, because, being young grownups, they would never survive it.

What your youngster has managed in the first step, *visual differentiation,* is very important.

Reading letters is very difficult since nobody ever ate an *a* or caught an *a* or wore an *a* or opened an *a.* One can eat a *banana,* catch a *ball,* wear a *shirt* or open a *book.* While the letters that make up the word "ball" are abstract, the ball itself is not and thus it is easier to learn the word "ball" than it is to learn the letter *b.*

Also the word "ball" is much more different from the word "nose" than the letter *a* is different from the letter *b.*

These two facts make words much easier to read than letters.

The letters of the alphabet are *not* the units of reading and writing any more than isolated sounds are the units of hearing and speaking. *Words* are the units of language. Letters are simply technical construction materials within words as clay, wood and rock are construction materials of a building. It is the bricks, boards and stones which are the true units of house construction.

Much later, when the child reads well, we will teach him the alphabet. By that time he will be able to see why it was necessary for man to invent an alphabet and why we need letters.

THE SECOND STEP (The "Self" Vocabulary)

We begin teaching a small child to read words by using the "self" words because the child learns first about his own body. His world begins inside and works gradually outside, a fact which educators have known for a long time.

A number of years ago a bright educator expressed by some magic letters something which did much to improve education. These letters were V.A.T.—visual, auditory, and tactile. It was pointed out that children learned through a combination of seeing (V), hearing (A), and feeling (T). And yet, mothers have always been playing and saying things like, "This little piggy went to market and this little piggy stayed home . . .", holding the toes up so the child could see them (visual), saying the words so the child could hear them (auditory), and squeezing the toes so the child could feel them (tactile).

In any event, we begin with the "self" words. They are smaller than the first words but still big, still lower case, and still red.

Like the previous words, these are introduced one at a time with the rest of the "self" words concealed.

Again the child should be in a good mood and his immediate environment as free from distracting factors as possible.

The "self" vocabulary contains the following twenty words, each on a white card 5″ high, in red lower-case letters 4″ high.

hand	leg	teeth	finger	shoulder
knee	eye	belly	tongue	
foot	ear	mouth		
head	arm	elbow		
nose		thumb		
hair				
lips				
toes				

You would now add two more sets of words to equal five sets of words in all, or twenty-five words divided into five sets. These two new sets should be taken from the "self" vocabulary.

Here is the system you should use from this point on in adding new words and taking out old ones:

Simply remove one word from each set that has already been taught for five days and replace the word with a new one in each set. Your child's first three sets have already been seen for a week so you may now begin to take out an old word in each set and put in a new one. Five days from now, retire an old word from each of the five sets you are presently using and add a new word to each set. Do this every day.

In summary then, you will be teaching twenty-five words daily, divided into five sets of five words each. Your child will be seeing five new words daily or one in each set, and five old words will be retired each day.

Avoid presenting consecutively two words that begin with the same letter. "Hair," "hand" and "head" all begin with "h" and therefore should not be taught consecutively. Occasionally a child will leap to the conclusion that *hair* is *hand* because the words both begin with "h" and are similar in appearance. Children who have already been taught the entire alphabet are much more likely to commit this error than children who do not know the alphabet. Knowing the alphabet causes minor confusion to the child. In teaching the word "arm," for example, mothers may experience the problem of a child's recognizing his old friend *a* and exclaiming over it, instead of reading the word *arm.*

Again one must remember the supreme rule of never boring the child. If he is bored there is a strong likelihood that you are going too slowly. He should be learning quickly and pushing you to play the game some more.

If you have done it well he will be averaging five new words daily. He may average ten new words a day. If you are clever enough and enthusiastic enough, he may learn more.

When your child has learned the "self" words, you are ready to move to the next step in the process of reading. He now has *two* of the most difficult steps in learning to read behind him. If he has succeeded up to now, you will find it difficult to prevent him from reading much longer.

However, before we move to the next step in teaching your child to read it is necessary to say something about the one-year-old who is learning to read but who does not yet talk.

If you start your child at one year old or before, he may not yet talk, or says only "mommy" and one or two other words. It is quite possible to be able to read before one is able to speak. We have seen thousands of children who can read thousands of words who can not yet talk.

Among adults it is almost always true that an adult can read a great deal more of a *new* language than he can understand of that language through his ear. Remember that a baby *is* learning a new language.

Let us suppose that you have decided to teach your six-month-old child to read. Absolutely fine, go right ahead. Do it in exactly the same manner in which you would teach a child who talks. It will be easier for the six-month-old but more difficult for you.

The obstacle here, of course, is that of testing. It is obvious that if a child is unable to say "hand," you will not be able to test him the same way you can an older child. When such is the case the parent will have to resort to more indirect testing measures and say to the child, "Where is the word 'hand'?" or "Give me the word 'hand.'"

If the parent of the nontalking child is willing to go to this small amount of extra effort he will find it rewarding.

Remember reading is not talking. We adults are apt to think the two are the same thing. This is both unfortunate and unwise. Tiny children are capable of reading before they can talk. A six-month-old can not say his name yet but he can most definitely recognize the reading card with his name on it if he has been shown it frequently. A sixteen-month-old speaks inconsistently and may or may not wish to say his reading words. A three year old, as everyone knows, does exactly and precisely what pleases him most. If he wishes to shout out his reading words he may do so, if he doesn't wish to say them he won't. The point is to teach your child, whatever his age, and recognize his right to demonstrate his knowledge in the way *he* chooses.

The fact that your child may be too young to speak or may not wish to say his reading words does not negate the fact that you are increasing and enriching his language by teaching him to read.

Indeed such investments in teaching the baby to read will *speed* his talking and broaden his vocabulary. Remember that language is language, whether transmitted to the brain via the eye or via the ear.

At The Institutes for the Achievement of Human Potential we use reading as one of the important means of teaching brain-injured children to speak.

THE THIRD STEP (The "Home" Vocabulary)

By now both parent and child should be approaching this game of reading with great pleasure and anticipation. Remember, you are building into your child a love of learning that will multiply throughout his life. More accurately, you are reinforcing a built-in rage for learning which will not be denied, but which can certainly be twisted into useless or even very negative channels in a child. Play the game with joy and enthusiasm.

The third step, teaching your child the "home" words, is merely a matter of continuing with additional nouns except that now they are the familiar objects of his surroundings.

The "home" words are smaller that the "self" words. They are still red, still lower-case letters, but now half the size of the "self" words. They are 2" high on cards 3" high.

The "home" vocabulary consists of those words that name the objects around him, such as "chair" and "wall."

It is wise at this point to talk about the rate at which each individual child should learn to read or, for that matter, to learn anything.

John Ciardi, writing in the May 11, 1963 issue of the *Saturday Review* said that a child should be fed new knowledge "at the rate determined by her own happy hunger." This, I think, sums up the situation beautifully.

Don't be afraid to follow the child's lead in this matter. You may be astonished at the size of his happy hunger and at the rate at which he learns.

The "home" vocabulary is actually divided into several subvocabularies. These are objects, possessions and "doing" groups.

Proper names which normally begin with a capital letter should be capitalized. It is neither necessary nor is it wise to bring the capital letter to the child's attention in any way. He will not question the capital letter unless he already knows the alphabet. If he already knows the alphabet and questions the capital letter, it will be necessary to explain briefly that names begin with capital letters.

By this time the child will have a reading vocabulary of twenty-five to thirty words and it will no longer be wise to review all the words he has learned. He will find this boring. Children love to learn but they do not love to be tested. Testing invariably introduces some degree of tension into the situation on the part of the parent, and children perceive this readily. They are likely to associate tension and unpleasantness with learning.

About once a week give your child an opportunity to show you what he knows *if he wishes to do so.*

Be sure to show your child how much you love and respect him at every opportunity.

A. Objects (these are family owned objects)

chair	table	door
window	wall	bedroom
bathroom	kitchcn	refrigerator
tv		

This list should also be added to or subtracted from to reflect the child's home surrounding and family-owned items which are special to his particular family.

Now continue to feed your child's happy hunger with the possessions words.

B. Possessions (objects that belong to the child himself)

plate	spoon
cup	hat
shoes	ball
orange	pants
dress	pajamas

As in the previous sub-vocabularies this list should be altered to reflect your child's own particular possessions and those things he or she loves the most. Obviously, the list will vary somewhat depending upon whether your child is eighteen months old or whether he is five years old.

Your child is taught the words in exactly the same way he has been taught up to now. This list can vary from ten words to fifty words, as the parent and the child choose.

The reading list (which up to this point may be approximately fifty words) has been composed entirely of nouns. The next grouping in the home vocabulary reflects action and consequently introduces verbs for the first time.

C. Doing

sitting	creeping
standing	walking
running	jumping
laughing	throwing
climbing	reading

For added fun with this set, as each new word is taught Mother first illustrates the act by (for example), jumping, and saying, "Mommy is jumping." She then has the child jump and says, "Billy is jumping." Mother now shows her child the word and says, "This word says 'jumping.'" In this way she goes through all the "doing" words. The child will particularly enjoy this, since it involves him, his mother (or father), action and learning.

When your child has learned the basic "home" words he is ready to move ahead.

By now your child is reading more than fifty words and both you and he should be delighted. Two points should be made before continuing to the next step, which is the beginning of the end in the process of learning to read.

If the parent has approached teaching his or her child to read as sheer pleasure (as should ideally be the case) rather than as a duty or obligation (which in the end is not a good enough reason), then both the parent and child should be enjoying themselves immensely in the daily sessions.

John Ciardi, in the editorial which has already been mentioned, said of the child, ". . . . . if he has been loved (which is basically to say, if he has been played with by parents who found honest pleasure in the play) . . . . .". This is a superb description of love—play *and* learning with a child—and it should never be far from a parent's mind while teaching a child to read.

The next point for a parent to remember is that children are vastly curious about words, whether written or spoken. When a child expresses interest in a word, for whatever reason, it is now wise to print it for him and add it to his vocabulary. He will read very quickly and easily any word that he has asked about.

Therefore, if a child should ask, "Mommy, what is a rhinoceros?" or "What does microscopic mean?" it is very wise to answer the question carefully and then print the word immediately, and so add it to his reading vocabulary.

He will feel a special pride and get additional pleasure from learning to read words which he himself generated.

THE FOURTH STEP (The
Sentence-Structure Vocabulary)

A chimpanzee can be taught to sit every time the word "sit" is shown to him.

However, it does not follow that he could now respond to a sentence in which words were used in a combination he had never seen before.

If we could understand only sentences that we had seen and known before, our "reading" would indeed be limited. All of the anticipation of opening a new book lies in finding what the book is going to say that we have never read before. To recognize individual words and to realize that they represent an object or an idea is a basic step in learning to read. To recognize that words, when used in a sentence, can represent a more complicated idea is an additional and vitally important step.

Up to this time your child has been exposed only to individual words, and since, as we have said, a primary method in learning is to go from the familiar to the unfamiliar, we begin this step also with individual words. These are even more important, because although your child does not know it, the individual words he learns now are those which in the Fifth Step will compose sentences. These same sentences will in the Sixth Step compose a book.

The parent will now need to procure the book which he will use to teach his child to read and from which he must work backward from the Sixth Step to the Fourth Step. The choice of the book to be used is very important and should meet the following standards:

a. It should have a vocabulary of not more than 150 words.
b. It should present no more than a total of 15 or 20 words on a single page.
c. The printing should be no less than ¼ " high.
d. Text and illustrations should be separated as much as possible.

While few books meet all of these requirements, there are some which come close to meeting all of them. Three examples are:

Goodbye Mommy, Bruce King Doman,
   THE BETTER BABY PRESS
   8801 Stenton Avenue, Philadelphia, Pa. 19118

Nose Is Not Toes, Glenn Doman
   THE BETTER BABY PRESS
   8801 Stenton Avenue, Philadelphia, Pa. 19118

The Path To Math, Greta Erdtmann
THE BETTER BABY PRESS
8801 Stenton Avenue, Philadelphia, Pa. 19118

Now cards must be prepared for the Fourth, Fifth, and Sixth Steps.

The parent takes each individual page of the book he has chosen and prints all of the words on that page on one card; these should be printed in black lowercase letters 1″ high. These become the "structured-phrase" cards which will be used in the Fifth Step. The parent will, as a result of having done this, end up with the same number of cards as there are written pages in the book. All the cards should be the same size, even though they don't all contain the same number of words.

The parent then prepares a card 3″ high and as long as required for the longest word used in the text (the Fourth Step). The letter should be black, lower-case and 2″ in height. Now the parent has the materials ready for the next steps.

Using the pages of the book to be read as a guide, the parent takes the individual words which appear on the first page of the book, and which are now in 2″ letters, and teaches them to the child in the order they appear. The parent uses the same method of teaching which was used with the other words up to this time. Each word is taught separately. Do not comment on the fact that these words are black instead of red.

It is also important not to try to explain or define the words to the child. While he uses the word "the" correctly in ordinary speech and therefore understands it, he does not deal with it as an isolated word. It is, of course, vital to reading that he *recognize* and *read* it as a separate word, but is is not necessary that he be able to define it. In the same way, all children speak correctly long before they know the rules of grammar. Besides, how would you like to explain what "the" means, even to a ten-year-old? So don't. Just be sure he can read it.

Assuming that the parent had decided to use the book *Goodbye Mommy* he would find that the first page contains the words "Here is Tommy." Therefore, these three words each appear in 2″ high, black lowercase letters on white cards 3″ high.

The parent starts with the word "here" and teaches the child this word in the same way that has been used before. Remember not to mention its definition. Just teach it as a new word as before. When the parent is confident that the child can identify this word the child is then ready to read the word "is". Following this the child is taught the word "Tommy".

When the parent is confident that the child knows

those three words we are ready for an important new step, the reading of words in relationship to one another.

The parent now takes the three words and places them, side by side and in their proper order, on the floor or on a table.

The parent then says slowly and clearly, "These three words together say "Here is Tommy." She points to each of them as she says it.

Reading several words together is a real challenge to the young child. It is most important that this step be carried out both carefully and joyfully. It is worth every bit of effort which may be required at this time. Some children accomplish this effortlessly and easily, others require a little longer, but if you are patient and very loud in your praise the child will win.

It is important that the child recognize the words individually before he recognizes them in grouping.

Just as it is true that words and not letters are the basic unit of language, it is also true that sentences are not the basic units of language. Sentences *are* language. It is not possible to understand written or spoken language without understanding the basic words which comprise language, but it *is* possible to understand language without defining individually the letters of the alphabet or the individual sounds that make up words. Your child is a splendid example of this since by this stage of the game he has successfully done *both* these things.

The caution that must be inserted here is against teaching him to read sentences without first teaching him to read the words within the sentences.

The child is now ready to learn the individual words which appear in the second sentence of the book the parent is using. The child, of course, has not seen the book and will not see it until a good deal later.

In the case of the book *Goodbye Mommy,* the words which appear in the second sentence are "and here is his Mommy".

In the same manner in which she taught the words of the first sentence, Mother then teaches the child the words of the second sentence.

Now Mother continues through the book, teaching the child every word individually that is contained in the text and then presenting all the words contained on each page together and in their proper order before advancing to the next page.

The time this takes per page will vary with the child, the mother and the number of words on the individual page. It should proceed no slower than the learning of five new words per day and probably could be much faster.

The book *Goodbye Mommy* contains a total of 81 different words, of which many are already familiar to the child, since they are words from the previous vocabulary. Therefore, in the entire book there are only about 62 words which are new to him. These 62 words are the "sentence-structure" vocabulary, if this is the book that the parent chooses.

There is no question that unless children can read individual words they are not reading. Be sure that your child reads the individual words as well as the groupings before continuing to the next step.

THE FIFTH STEP (Structured Phrases and Sentences)

This step is quite easy because, in a sense, it is already accomplished. It is exciting, too, because when it is finished the child will have actually read a book. It will be a little book and a make-it-yourself book, but a book nevertheless.

In the book *Goodbye Mommy* there are 51 pages containing a phrase, or a sentence. Therefore, there will now be 51 cards, each listing the words that appear on each page of the book. In addition, the cards have holes punched at one end so that they may be placed on looseleaf rings, which may be purchased in any stationery store.

The child has actually already read every one of these phrases and sentences but has read the words on individual cards and in letters twice as large.

Now the real fun begins. Starting with the first card the parent teaches in exactly the same manner she has employed in the past. She should proceed at the rate of five new cards a day.

The first card contains the words "Here is Tommy;" the second card, "and here is his Mommy;" the third card, "His Mommy is going," and so on through all the pages of the book.

Holding up the first card the parent reads slowly and clearly, "Here is Tommy".

When each of these cards has been shown three times daily for five days you can be sure your child knows them well. When this is accomplished each page is ceremoniously placed into the looseleaf rings. Again this is a proper time to celebrate.

In this way the child's book multiplies at the rate of about five pages each day, and if all goes well at the end of 18 days, the child will have a complete make-it-yourself book. If this proves too slow for a particular child, the rate should by all means be accelerated.

As each new page is added the previous pages are reread.

The last stage of this procedure is the awarding of a certificate bearing mother's signature testifying that on this date and at this age her child has completed reading his first book.

It is quite an accomplishment.

You may properly be very proud of each other— you and your child.

THE SIXTH STEP (Reading a Real Book)

Now your child is ready to read a real and proper book. The fact is that he has already done so twice, once with the separate words on cards and once with the complete sentences on loose card pages. The only thing that is different really is that the words, phrases and sentences of the book which he already knows are now in black upper and lower-case letters and only ¼″ high.

However, the difference between the 2″ letters of the Fourth Step, the 1″ letters of the Fifth Step and the ¼″ letters of the Sixth Step can be a very important one if the child is very young. Remember that as you have taught him to read, you have actually been helping to mature and improve his visual pathway.

In the event you are moving faster than your child's visual apparatus is able to mature, you will have a clear-cut indication of this during the Fourth, Fifth and Sixth Steps.

Since the words he is using in these last three steps are exactly the same words but differ only in the fact that they become smaller with each step, you can now see quite clearly if a child is learning faster than his visual pathway is able to mature.

As an example, suppose that a child completes the Fourth and Fifth Steps successfully but has difficulty in reading the identical words in the book itself. The solution is simple. We know that the child can read 1″ words easily. Now the parent simply prepares additional words and simple sentences 1″ in height. Use simple, imaginative words and sentences which the child will enjoy reading, and after two months of this, return again to the book.

Remember that if the print were made too small you would also have trouble reading it.

If the child is three years of age by the time you get to the ¼″ print of the book itself, you will probably not be held up at all at this point. If the child is less than two years old by the time you get to the book, there is a fairly good chance that you will need to obtain or create additional 1″ or 2″ letters for the child. Fine, it is all reading, and real reading at that. It will mature his brain growth far more than would otherwise be the case.

Now have your child read the real book—word, phrase, sentence and page at a time—making no effort to conceal your delight with the fact that he can do so. The child will seldom accomplish a more important act in all the life that is ahead of him.

Believe it or not, your child has read a book, and if you started early enough and were properly appreciative, joyful and enthusiastic he may not yet have reached his second birthday.

THE SEVENTH STEP (The Alphabet)

You are now an expert teacher—you have taught a tiny child to read—and up to the time of the publication of this book only a small percentage of people have done so.

Come to think of it, who are *we* to tell *you* how to teach a child to learn the alphabet? Using whatever system and materials you think are wise, teach him the alphabet—both upper and lower case. It will be far easier now.

It is also quite possible that by now he has learned

much of the alphabet, or even all of it, without any help from us or you.

There are three distinct levels of understanding in the process of learning how to read. As the child conquers each of them he will show exuberance at his new and very exciting discovery. The joy Columbus must have known in finding a new world could hardly have been greater than that which the child will experience at each stage of these breakthroughs.

Naturally, his first pleasure and delight is in the disclosure that words have meaning. To the child this is almost like a secret code which he shares with grownups. He will enjoy this vastly and visibly.

Next he notices that the words he reads can be used together and are therefore more than merely labels for objects. This is also a new and wonderful revelation.

The last discovery he makes will probably be very noticeable to the parent. This, the greatest of them all, is that the book which he is reading represents more than the simple fun of translating secret names into objects, and more even than the decoding of strings of words into comments about objects and people. Suddenly and delightfully the big secret bursts upon the child that this book is actually talking to him, and to him alone.

When the child comes to this realization (and this does not necessarily happen in his first or second book), there will be no stopping him. He will now be a reader in every sense of the word. He now realizes that the words he already knows can be rearranged to make entirely new ideas. He does not have to learn a new set of words every time he has to read something.

What a discovery this is! Few things will compare to it in later life. He can now have an adult talking to him in a new conversation any time he wants, simply by picking up a new book.

All of man's knowledge is now available to him. Not only the knowledge of people he knows in his home and neighborhood, but people far away whom he will never see. Even more than that, he can be approached by people who lived long ago in other places and in other ages.

Human beings are the only creatures on earth who can alter the evolutionary pathway. Most creatures in the evolutionary march toward man are now extinct. Others played their roles and did not disappear but instead remained to mark time in place forever.

This power to control our own fate began, as we shall see, with our ability to write and to read. Because man has been able to write and to read he has been able to pass on to other men centuries later and in remote places the knowledge he has gained. Man's knowledge is cumulative.

Man is man essentially because he can read and write.

This is the true importance of what your child discovers when he learns to read. The child may even try, in his own way, to tell you about his great discovery, lest you, his parent, miss it. If he does, listen to him respectfully and with love. What he has to say is important.

There isn't anything more that needs saying in this chapter except to give you a list of books for further reading.

They are listed in the order in which they should be read, and were chosen for several characteristics:

1. Large enough print.
2. Print not intertwined with pictures.
3. Size of vocabulary.
4. Subject matter.

Any book chosen has to meet each of those requirements to one degree or another.

The child began his first book with a reading vocabulary of about 50 words.

By now he should have a reading vocabulary of

close to 100 words or even more.

The books we suggest he reads next are the titles that follow.

All are available through the Better Baby Press.

SUGGESTED TITLES FOR FURTHER READING:

Which Composer?
Janet Doman and Susan Aisen

What Reptile?
Janet Doman and Susan Aisen

What Bird?
Janet Doman and Susan Aisen

Which President?
Janet Doman and Susan Aisen

What Insect?
Janet Doman and Susan Aisen

Remember the Runcible Spoon.
Janet Doman and Susan Aisen

8

on joyousness

I don't think we really got to know each other until we played the learning-to-read game together.

—MANY, MANY MOTHERS

For many generations grandparents have been advising their sons and daughters to enjoy their children because, they have warned, all too soon the children will be grown-up and gone. Like much good advice that has been passed on from one generation to another it is rarely heeded until it has happened. When it has happened it is, of course, too late to do anything about it.

If it is true that the parents of brain-injured

children have monumental problems (and they certainly do), it is equally true that they have certain advantages that the parents of well children rarely have. Not the least of these advantages is the fact that they have a very intimate relationship with their children. By the nature of the illness it is sometimes an agonizing one, but it is also a precious one.

Recently, during a course we were presenting to the parents of well children on the subject of how to teach your baby to read, we said in passing, "And another excellent reason for teaching your baby to read is the fact that in the close relationship required you will experience a great deal of the joy that the parents of brain-injured children know in dealing with their children."

It was not until several sentences further along that we became aware of the puzzled looks that our comments had produced.

It is not surprising that parents of well children are not aware of the fact that the parents of brain-injured children have some advantages and not only problems. It is surprising, however, that the vast majority of us have lost the constant and intimate relationship with our children that is so important to the child's entire future and which can be so splendidly pleasurable to us.

The pressures of our society and of our culture have robbed us of this so quietly that we have been unaware of the fact that it is gone, or perhaps we have been unaware that it ever existed.

It did exist, and it is worth recapturing. One of the most rewarding ways to recapture this joyous association is by teaching your baby to read.

Now that you know how to do it, let's finish off with some final reminders—some do's and some don'ts.

Let's begin with the don'ts.

Don't bore your child

It is the cardinal sin. Remember that the two-year-old could be learning Portuguese and French along with the English he is learning so well. So don't bore him with trivia and drivel. There are three easy ways to bore him. Avoid them like the plague.

a. *Going too fast* will bore him, because if you go too fast he won't be learning and he wants to learn. (This is the least likely way of boring him, since very few people go too fast.)

b. *Going too slow* will bore him, because he will learn at a surprising rate. Many people commit this sin in their desire to be quite positive he knows the material.

c. *Testing him too much* is the most likely sin and this will surely bore him. Children love to learn but they do not love to be tested. This is the primary reason why all the commotion is called for after he has tested successfully.

Two factors precipitate toward too much testing. The first of these is the naturally proud parent showing off the child's abilities to neighbors, cousins, grandparents, and so on. The second factor is the parent's keen desire to be *sure* he reads each word perfectly before moving on to the next step. Remember that you are not giving your child college board examinations, you're simply giving him an opportunity to learn to read. It is not necessary to prove to the world that he can read. (He'll prove it all by himself later on.) Only *you* need be sure, and parents have special, built-in equipment for knowing what their children know and what they don't. Trust that equipment and the judgment it hands down. That special equipment is made up of equal portions of head and heart, and when both of these things are in total accord you get a good verdict almost invariably.

We shall not soon forget a conversation with an outstanding pediatric neurosurgeon who was discussing a severely brain-injured child. The brain surgeon was a man whose every instinct was based on deliberate, almost cold-blooded scientific evidence.

He was talking about a fifteen-year-old severely brain-injured child, paralyzed and speechless, who had been diagnosed as an idiot. The doctor was furious. "Look at this child," he insisted. "He has been diagnosed as an idiot simply because he looks like an idiot, acts like an idiot, and the laboratory tests indicate that he is an idiot. Anyone should be able to see that he is not an idiot."

There was a long, embarrassed, somewhat frightened silence among the residents, internes, nurses and therapists who composed the brain surgeon's retinue. Finally a resident, bolder than the rest, said, "But, Doctor, if everything indicates that this child is an idiot, how do you know that he isn't?"

"Good God," roared the scientist-surgeon, "look at his eyes, man, you don't need any special training to see the intelligence shining in them!"

A year later we were privileged to watch that child walk, talk and read for the same group of people.

There are accurate ways for parents to know what a child knows outside of the realm of the ordinary tests.

If you repeat too often a test which a child has already passed, he will become bored and will reply by telling you he doesn't know or by giving you an absurd answer. If you show a child the word "hair" and ask him too often what it is, he may tell you that it is "elephant." When he replies in this way your child is straightening you out by reproof. Pay attention to him.

Don't pressure your child

Don't cram reading down his throat. Don't be *determined* to teach him to read. Don't be afraid of failure. (How can you fail? If he only learns three words he will be better off than if he knows none at all.) You must *not* give him the opportunity to learn to read if either one of you doesn't feel like doing it. Teaching a child to read is a very positive thing and you must never make it negative. If the child doesn't want to play at any time during the learning process, put the whole thing away for a week or so. Remember you have absolutely nothing to lose and everything to gain.

Don't be tense

If you are not relaxed, don't play the game by attempting to cover up your tension. A child is the most sensitive instrument imaginable. He will know that you are tense and that will subtly convey unpleasantness to him. It is much better to waste a day or a week. Never try to fool the child. You won't succeed.

Don't teach the alphabet first

Unless your child has already learned the alphabet, don't teach it to him until he has finished reading his first book. Doing so will tend to make him a slower reader than he would otherwise be. He will tend to read the letters instead of the words. Remember that words and not letters are the basic units of language. If he already knows the alphabet you can still teach him to read. Kids are wonderfully pliable.

That about sums up the things you shouldn't do.

Now let's look at the things you should do, because they are even more important.

Be joyous

We have said earlier in this book that thousands of parents and scientists have taught children to read and that the results have been splendid.

We have read about these people, we have corresponded with many of these people, and we have talked to many of them. We have found that the methods they employ have varied widely. They have used materials ranging from pencil and paper to complex scientific machines which cost more than a third of a million dollars. However, and most significantly, each of the methods about which we have learned had three things in common, and they are of the utmost importance.

a. Each method used in teaching tiny children to read was successful.
b. Each of them used large letters.
c. Each of them stressed the absolute necessity for feeling and expressing joyousness in the process.

The first two points surprised us not at all, but the third point astonished us.

It must be remembered that the many people teaching children to read were unaware of one another, and that they were often generations apart.

It is not just a coincidence that all of them came to the conclusion that a child should be rewarded for his success by lavish praise. They would have had to come to that conclusion sooner or later.

What is truly astonishing is that people working in 1914, 1918, 1962 and 1963 and in other times and far-flung places should all have come to the conclusion that this attitude should be summed up in a single, identical word—*joyous*.

To almost the precise degree that a parent's attitude is joyous will he succeed in teaching his child to read.

There was a strong temptation to title this final chapter of the book "The Dizzy Blondes," and thereby hangs a brief but important tale.

Through the years, we at The Institutes have gained a vast respect for mothers. Like most people we have erred by making easy generalizations and have therefore, at least for convenience, divided the thousands of mothers with whom we have had the privilege of dealing, into two categories. The first category is a relatively small group of highly intellectual, highly educated, very calm, very quiet, and generally, but not invariably, intelligent mothers. This group we have termed "the intellectuals."

The second group is by far the largest and includes almost everybody else. While these women are often intelligent, they are inclined to be less intellectual and a good deal more enthusiastic than the first. This group of mothers we have called "the dizzy blondes," which reflects their enthusiasm rather than the color of their hair or their intelligence.

Like all generalizations the above doesn't hold up, but it does make for rapid grouping.

When we first became aware that mothers could teach their tiny children to read and that this was a fine thing to do we said to each other, "Wait till our mothers hear about this." We anticipated correctly that all of our mothers would be delighted and that they would tackle this process with enthusiasm.

We came to the conclusion that the vast majority of mothers would be successful in teaching their children to read, but we predicted that the small group of intellectuals would enjoy even more success than "the dizzy blondes."

When the first results of the early experiments began to come in, almost exactly the opposite of what we had anticipated proved to be the case. All later results confirmed and reconfirmed our initial findings.

All of the mothers had succeeded beyond our initial expectations but "the dizzy blondes" were well ahead of the intellectuals, and the dizzier the mother the more she accomplished.

When we examined the results, watched the process, listened to the mother and thought about it all for a while, the reasons for the whole thing became obvious.

When the quiet, serious mother asked her child to read a word or a sentence, and the child did it well, the intellectual mother was inclined to say, "That's splendid, Mary, now what is this next word?"

On the other hand, the mothers who approached their children less intellectually were a great deal more inclined to shout "Wow! That's great!" when a child succeeded. These were the mothers who showed by voice, motion and commotion their elation with the child's success.

Again the answer was simple. Tiny children understand, appreciate and go for "Wow!" a great deal more than they go for carefully chosen words of praise. Children dig celebrations—so give them what they want. They deserve it and so do you.

There are so many things we parents *must* do for our children. We must take care of all of their problems, the occasional large serious ones and the innumerable smaller ones. Both the kids and we are entitled to some joy and that's just what teaching them to read is—a joy.

But if the idea of teaching your child to read doesn't appeal to you, don't do it. No one should teach his child to read just for the sake of keeping up with the Joneses. If you feel that way, you'll be a bad teacher. If you want to do it, then do it because you want to—that's a splendid reason.

If we must deal with all the problems our children have, then we should also have the pleasures that go with this instead of turning such opportunities for happiness over to strangers. What a privilege it is to open, for a child, a door which has behind it all of the golden words of excitement, splendor and wonder which are contained in the books of the English language. That's much too good to be turned over to a stranger. That joyous privilege should be reserved for Mom or Dad.

Be inventive.

Long ago we learned that if you tell mothers what the objective is in any project related to their kids, and if you then tell them in general how it should be done, you can stop worrying about it right then and there. Parents are extraordinarily inventive and as long as they know what the limits are, they will often come up with better methods than they have been told to use.

Every child shares many characteristics with all other children (and chief among them is the ability to learn to read at a very early age), but every child is also very much an individual. He is a product of his family, his life and his home. Because they are all different, there are many small games that Mom can and will invent to make learning to read more fun for her child. Obey the rules, but go ahead and add things that you know will work particularly well for your child. Don't be afraid to tamper within the framework of rules which have been set forth here.

Answer all of the child's questions.

He will have a thousand questions. Answer them seriously and as accurately as you can. You opened a large door when you taught him to read. Don't be surprised at the vast number of things which will interest him. The most common question you will hear from now on is, "What is this word?" That's how he'll learn to read all the books from now on. Always tell him what that word is. His basic reading vocabulary will grow at a very rapid rate if you do.

Give him worth-while material to read.

There are so many magnificent things to read that there should be very little time devoted to junk.

Perhaps the most important thing overall is that reading gives you the opportunity to spend more time in personal, close and intriguing contact with your child. Take advantage of every opportunity to be with your child. Modern living has tended to pull mothers and children apart. Here is the perfect chance to get together. The mutual love, respect and admiration which will grow greater through such contact is worth many, many times over the small amounts of time which you will have to spend.

It seems worth-while to finish by speculating briefly on what all this could mean to the future.

All through history man has had two dreams. The first of these dreams, and the simpler, has been to change the world around us for the better. We have succeeded in doing this to a fantastic degree.

At the turn of the century man could travel no faster than a little over a hundred miles per hour. Today he is capable of flying through space at more than 17,000 miles per hour. We have developed miracle drugs which will double man's life span. We have learned how to project our voices and our images through space by radio and television. Our buildings are truly miracles of height, beauty, warmth and comfort. We have changed the world around us in the most extraordinary way.

But what of man himself? He lives longer because he has invented better medicine. He grows taller because the transportation he has invented brings him a greater variety of food, and therefore nutrition, from distant places.

But is man himself better? Are there men of greater imaginative genius than Da Vinci? Are there better writers than Shakespeare? Are there men with further vision and broader knowledge than Franklin and Jefferson?

Since time immemorial there have been men who fostered the second dream. For ages some men have dared to ask the question, "But what of man himself?" As the world around us daily grows more breath-takingly complex, we have need for a new, better and wiser breed of man.

People have, of necessity, grown more specialized and narrow. There is no longer time enough to know everything. Yet ways must be found to cope with the situation, to give more people the opportunity of gaining the tremendous amount of knowledge man has accumulated.

We cannot solve this problem by going to school forever. Who will run the world or be the bread-winner?

Making man live longer doesn't really help this particular problem. If even a genius like Einstein had lived five years longer, would he have contributed much more to the world's knowledge? It is unlikely. Longevity does not contribute to creativity.

The answer to this problem may already have occurred to you. Suppose more children were introduced to the great storehouse of knowledge accumulated by man four or five years earlier then they are now? Imagine the result if Einstein could have had five extra years of creative life. Imagine what might happen if children could begin to absorb the wisdom and knowledge of the world, years before they are now allowed to?

What a race and what a future might we not produce if we could stop the tragic waste of children's lives when their ability to take in language in all forms is at its peak.

Certainly it is no longer a question whether very young children can read or not, it is now only a question of what they are going to read.

The real question, we guess, now that the secret

is out and all that, is a new one. Now that the kids can read and thus increase their knowledge, perhaps beyond anybody's wildest dreams—what will they do with this old world and how tolerant will they be with us old parents, who by their standards may be nice—but perhaps not very bright?

It was said long ago, and said wisely, that the pen is mightier than the sword. We must, I think, accept the belief that knowledge leads to greater understanding and thus to greater good, while ignorance inevitably leads to evil.

Little children have begun to read and thus to increase their knowledge, and if this book leads to only one child reading sooner and better, then it will have been worth the effort. Who can say what another superior child will mean to the world? Who is to say what, in the end, will be the sum total of good for man as a result of this quiet ground swell which has already begun, this gentle revolution.

acknowledgments

Nobody ever writes a book all by himself; behind every work stretches a long line of the people who made it possible. In the immediate past these people are in sharp focus, but as the line gets farther back the image of those who contributed gets dimmer and is finally totally obscured by the fog of time itself. Others go unsung, since many who have contributed to an idea have themselves passed into total obscurity.

Surely the lineal descent of this work passes back into time dimly seen and must include those who contributed even a single sentence or idea which helped complete the puzzle. It must finally include a host of mothers who knew in their hearts and minds that their children could do more than the world believed possible.

In short, in addition to those here acknowledged individually I wish to acknowledge all those in history who have believed with a consuming passion that children were really quite superior to the image that we adults have always held.

Among these many I acknowledge:

Dr. Temple Fay, a dean of neurosurgeons, who had a monumental curiosity and a unique ability to question whether accepted "truths" were true or not, and who first set us afire.

Mary Blackburn, the eternal secretary, who lived for the Children's Clinic and who, it may be said, died for it.

Dr. Eugene Spitz, pediatric neurosurgeon, who believes that "there is no more radical an act than watching a child die, knowing he is going to die and doing nothing about it." He has done so much about it.

Dr. Robert Doman, pediatric physiatrist and Medical Director of The Institutes for the Achievement of Human Potential, who wanted us to look at every single child as unique.

Dr. Raymundo Veras, physiatrist of Brazil, who returned to teach the teachers.

Dr. Carl Delacato, Director of The Institute of Reading Disability, who kept us ever mindful of the children.

Dr. Edward B. LeWinn, Director of The Research Institute, who insisted that we look at cerebrospinal fluid for the evidence we needed.

Florence Scott, R.N., who cared so much about children and who talked to them in a unique way.

Lindley Boyer, Director of The Rehabilitation Center at Philadelphia, who never stopped pushing to get our work done.

Greta Erdtmann, executive secretary, who gave me seclusion when I needed it.

Betty Milliner, whose work was exacting.

Behind all this team there have been those who cared and supported us through the days of obscurity and quest.

Helen Clarke, Herbert Thiel, Dora Kline Valentine, Gene Brog, Lloyd Wells, Frank McCormick, Robert Magee, Hugh Clarke, Gilbert Clarke, Harry Valentine, Edward and Dorothy Cassard, General Arthur Kemp, Hannah Cooke, Frank Cliffe, Chatham Wheat, Anthony Flores, Trimble Brown, Adjutant General of Pennsylvania Thomas R. White, Jr., Edward and Pat O'Donnell, Theodore Donahue, Harold McCuen, John and Mary Begley, Claude Cheek, Martin Palmer, Signe Brunnstromm, Agnes Seymour, Betty Marsh, Dr. Walter McKinney, Judge Summerill, George Leyrer, Raymond Schwartz, Ralph Rosenberg, Charlotte Kornbluh, Alan Emlen, David Taylor, Brooke Simcox, William Reimer, Emily Abell, Doris Magee, Joseph Barnes, Norma Hoffman, Tom and Sidney Carroll, Bea Lipp, Miles and Stuart Valentine, Morton Berman, John Gurt and a host of others.

The Medical Advisory Board who have, to a man, supported the work. The following physicians who have contributed to and whole-heartedly supported the work.

Dr. Thaine Billingsley, Dr. Charles DeLone, Dr. Paul Dunn, Dr. David Lozow, Dr. William

Ober, Dr. Robert Tentler, Dr. Myron Segal and Dr. Richard Darnell.

My children Bruce, Janet, and Douglas, who have contributed both inspirationally and materially to this book.

Robert Loomis, my editor, who dealt with me patiently and tactfully.

Last of all I acknowledge those superb teachers, the children, who have taught me most of all, especially Tommy Lunski and Walter Rice.

about the
author

GLENN J. DOMAN graduated from the University of Pennsylvania School of Physical Therapy in 1940, and then became a staff member of the Temple University Hospital in Philadelphia. He entered the United States Army as a private in 1941 and retired a lieutenant colonel, having been awarded the D.S.C., the Silver Star, the Bronze Star, the British Military Cross, and other decorations.

In his chosen field he has received the Roberto Simonsen Award from Brazil for his contributions to social science in that nation, the Gold Medal of Honor of Brazil, and others. He is now the Director of The Institutes for the Achievement of Human Potential at Philadelphia.